HE Loves TO Help YOU

PRAYER JOURNAL

ARLEEN GEATHERS

WESTBOW
PRESS®
A DIVISION OF THOMAS NELSON
& ZONDERVAN

WestBow Press books may be ordered through booksellers or by contacting:

WestBow Press
A Division of Thomas Nelson & Zondervan
1663 Liberty Drive
Bloomington, IN 47403
www.westbowpress.com
844-714-3454

ISBN: 978-1-6642-9125-6 (sc)
ISBN: 978-1-6642-9127-0 (hc)
ISBN: 978-1-6642-9126-3 (e)

Library of Congress Control Number: 2023905942

Print information available on the last page.

WestBow Press rev. date: 5/4/2023

Inspirational Journals 4 U is a collection of Christian journals that inspire you to use the power of your written voice to create for yourself a healthier mind, body and spirit.

"The Lord is Your Help" Prayer Journal inspires journalers to "pray through the pen". The scriptures throughout the journal will help you to focus on the greatness of GOD and how much HE loves to help you in times of trouble and growth. As you combine the strength of journaling your prayers, with the power of God's Word, you will inject faith, hope and good works into your challenging circumstances.

The cry for Help is not just a one-word prayer for action but also the calling out of the mighty name of the Holy Spirit. The Holy Spirit helps us by teaching us the truth. When navigating rough waters, this truth (1) serves as a guiding light, (2) leads us to Godly perspectives, (3) offers emotional stability and (4) reveals the perfect work of God's power and love. When possible, remember to journal the full life of your prayers: the circumstance or scripture that prompted the prayer, the prayer itself, the promise, the process, the answer and your gratitude.

The journal prompt at the top of each page is there for your pondering. You can use it as the focal point of your prayer or leap over it and get "write" into journaling.

I pray that after time and seasons have passed, you will look back through this journal and declare like David in Psalms 34:6 "this poor man cried and THE LORD HELPED him and delivered him out of all his troubles".

HELP

To make it possible for someone to have a victorious experience that would not have been accomplished without someone offering one's self, abilities, services, resources, authority, prayers, influence, power, voice, strength, sacrifice, encouragement, truth, instructions, wisdom, mercy, mentoring, understanding, forgiveness, faith, hope and love...

THE LORD IS YOUR HELP

Psalm 118:13-14 (ICB)

They chased me until I was almost defeated. But the Lord helped me. The Lord gives me strength and makes me sing. He has saved me. *(Replace the word "they" at the beginning of this Bible verse with something or someone relative to you and repeat it out loud: for example Grief and Depression chased me...)*

Contents

Daddy Will Help You

"Daddy I can't reach it!" was the declaration of Hannah. The three year old, who had somehow managed to kneel her way up the steps that lead to the Bankers Museum Park playground slide. Hannah's Dad, poised at a leapable distance from his daughter, smiled, as he watched carefully over Hannah conquest. He took much pleasure observing Hannah workout her faith by conquering one step and than another. Hannah was able to climb all the steps that led to the top of the slide, except the last one: it was more elevated than the others. Because Hannah's Daddy was watching her entire journey, he had already began moving toward her before she even cried out: "Daddy I can't reach it!" When she cried out, he instantly responded, **"Daddy will help you."**

> How often have we cried out to our Heavenly
> Father saying? "Daddy I can't reach it!"

I can't reach the peace spoken about in your Word; it seems this storm is too much
I can't reach your comfort I so desperately need after the loss of my loved one
I can't reach the hope needed to try again after another failure
I can't reach the forgiveness that is necessary to renovate my marriage
I can't reach the belief that my faith needs in order to experience healing
I can't reach my next… because there is a mountain of lack before me
I can't reach rest… because fighting is what I do best

In His Chambers

Daddy Will Help You

I can't reach good thoughts… because I keep rewinding the evil that happen to me

I can't reach the promise because I am exhausted from the journey

Daddy I need Your Help!
I Can't Reach It!

In the midst of so many I can'ts God says, "With man this is impossible, but with God all things are possible" **(Mark 10:27b)**.

Our Father, who knows all things, is

already positioned to help

already equipped with the best response to help

already able to perform the help

already full of power to help

already willing to help

and HE already knows you need help

before you even ask

GOD ALMIGHTY, who is our Daddy, when HE hears the prayers of HIS children crying Abba, "I can't reach it!" HE says:

"Daddy Will HELP You!"

In His Chambers

Mathew 6:8b-9a (ICB)

Your Father knows the things you need before you ask him. So when you pray, you should pray like this: "Our Father in heaven…"

Help me ask for help...
sometimes we do not have help because we have not asked for help

Date:_____

_____

_____

_____

_____

_____

_____

_____

_____

_____

_____

_____

_____

_____

_____

_____

_____

_____

_____

_____

In His Chambers

John 15:16 (NIV)

You did not choose me, but I chose you and appointed you so that you might go and bear fruit—fruit that will last—and so that whatever you ask in my name the Father will give you.

God shall hear...
Psalm 55:19a (KJV)

Date:_____

_____

_____

_____

_____

_____

_____

_____

_____

_____

_____

_____

_____

_____

_____

_____

_____

_____

_____

_____

_____

_____

_____

_____

_____

_____

_____

_____

_____

_____

In His Chambers

I do not want to ask for Help but I know I need it...

help me be humble and not prideful

Date:_____

_____

_____

_____

_____

_____

_____

_____

_____

_____

_____

_____

_____

_____

_____

_____

_____

In His Chambers

Psalm 116:1-2 (NIV)

I love the Lord, for he heard my voice; he heard my cry for mercy. Because he turned his ear to me, I will call on him as long as I live.

Let us then approach God's throne of grace with confidence, so that we may receive mercy and find grace to help us in our time of need...

Hebrews 4:16 (NIV)

Date:_____

_____

_____

_____

_____

_____

_____

_____

_____

_____

_____

_____

_____

_____

_____

_____

_____

_____

_____

_____

_____

_____

In His Chambers

Help me fuel my faith...
With good plans, intentional pursuit and obedient labor

Date:_____

_____

_____

_____

_____

_____

_____

_____

_____

_____

_____

_____

_____

_____

_____

_____

_____

In His Chambers

2 Peter 1:5-7 (ICB)

Because you have these blessings, you should try as much as you can to add these things to your lives: to your faith, add goodness; and to your goodness, add knowledge; and to your knowledge, add self-control; and to your self-control, add the ability to hold on; and to your ability to hold on, add service for God; and to your service for God, add kindness for your brothers and sisters in Christ; and to this kindness, add love.

Help me to agree with YOUR scriptures...

so that I can walk by faith and in harmony with YOU

Date:_____

_____

_____

_____

_____

_____

_____

_____

_____

_____

_____

_____

_____

_____

_____

_____

In His Chambers

2 Timothy 3:15-17 (ICB)

...The Scriptures are able to make you wise. And that wisdom leads to salvation through faith in Christ Jesus. All Scripture is inspired by God and is useful for teaching and for showing people what is wrong in their lives. It is useful for correcting faults and teaching how to live right. Using the Scriptures, the person who serves God will be ready and will have everything he needs to do every good work.

Hear, O Lord, and have mercy upon me: Lord, be thou my helper...

Psalm 30:10 (KJV)

Date:_____

_____

_____

_____

_____

_____

_____

_____

_____

_____

_____

_____

_____

_____

_____

_____

_____

_____

_____

_____

In His Chambers

Help me to know that my best defense is to TRUST IN THE LORD
and follow HIS lead
and remain under HIS wings

Date:_____

_____

_____

_____

_____

_____

_____

_____

_____

_____

_____

_____

_____

_____

_____

_____

_____

In His Chambers

1 Peter 5:8-9 (TLB)

Be careful—watch out for attacks from Satan, your great enemy. He prowls around like a hungry, roaring lion, looking for some victim to tear apart. Stand firm when he attacks. Trust the Lord; and remember that other Christians all around the world are going through these sufferings too.

Help me wait on YOU...
I have traveled too far and
have waited too long to drop out

Date:_____

_____
_____
_____
_____
_____
_____
_____
_____
_____
_____
_____
_____
_____
_____
_____
_____

In His Chambers

Isaiah 40:29-31(ICB)

The Lord gives strength to those who are tired. He gives more power to those who are weak. Even boys become tired and need to rest. Even young men trip and fall. But the people who trust the Lord will become strong again. They will be able to rise up as an eagle in the sky. They will run without needing rest. They will walk without becoming tired...

Help me not be frustrated...
while I am waiting on the Almighty,
all knowing and all powerful
God: who loves me

Date:_____

_____

_____

_____

_____

_____

_____

_____

_____

_____

_____

_____

_____

_____

_____

_____

_____

_____

_____

_____

In His Chambers

Psalm 27:14 (ICB)

I truly believe I will live to see the Lord's goodness. Wait for the Lord's help. Be strong and brave and wait for the Lord's help.

Jesus is your Help...
Jesus is my Help!
Jesus is our Help!

Date:_____

_____
_____
_____
_____
_____
_____
_____
_____
_____
_____
_____
_____
_____
_____
_____
_____
_____
_____

In His Chambers

Luke 18:38 (ICB)

The blind man cried out, "Jesus, Son of David! Please help me!"

Psalm 33:20 (NIV)

We wait in hope for the Lord; he is our help and our shield.

Lord, many thanks to YOU for helping!!!

Write a thank you note to Jesus for helping you move from worse to better, from good to better, or from better to the best.

Date:_____

_____

_____

_____

_____

_____

_____

_____

_____

_____

_____

_____

_____

_____

_____

_____

_____

_____

_____

_____

_____

_____

In His Chambers

Help me to remember I am precious...

to YOU

Date:_____

_____

_____

_____

_____

_____

_____

_____

_____

_____

_____

_____

_____

_____

_____

_____

In His Chambers

Psalm 139:17-18a (ICB)

God, your thoughts are precious to me. They are so many! If I could count them, they would be more than all the grains of sand.

Help me know that all I need to do is ask YOU...

for Godly wisdom direction, truth and help

Date:_____

_____

_____

_____

_____

_____

_____

_____

_____

_____

_____

_____

_____

_____

_____

_____

_____

_____

In His Chambers

James 4:2 (ICB)

You want things, but you do not have them. So you are ready to kill and are jealous of other people. But you still cannot get what you want. So you argue and fight. You do not get what you want because you do not ask God.

I see my help when I...
call on YOUR great name
sing YOUR praises
trust YOUR love
rest in YOUR sovereignty
meditate on YOUR goodness

Date:_____

_____

_____

_____

_____

_____

_____

_____

_____

_____

_____

_____

_____

_____

_____

_____

In His Chambers

Psalm 22:5 (TLB)

You heard their cries for help and saved them; they were never disappointed when they sought your aid.

Lord Help!

That is my hope
That is my prayer

Date:_____

_____

_____

_____

_____

_____

_____

_____

_____

_____

_____

_____

_____

_____

_____

_____

_____

_____

_____

_____

_____

_____

In His Chambers

2 Kings 13:4 (NLT)

Then Jehoahaz prayed for the Lord's help, and the Lord heard his prayer...

HELP!

I have made a mess of things again

Date:_____

_____

_____

_____

_____

_____

_____

_____

_____

_____

_____

_____

_____

_____

_____

_____

_____

_____

In His Chambers

Psalm 14:2 (ICB)

The Lord looked down from heaven at all the people. He looked to see if anyone was wise, if anyone was looking to God for help.

As for me, I will call upon God...

Psalm 55:16a (KJV)

Date:_____

_____

_____

_____

_____

_____

_____

_____

_____

_____

_____

_____

_____

_____

_____

_____

_____

_____

_____

_____

_____

_____

_____

_____

In His Chambers

Help me see the evidence that YOU are with me...

especially when I can not sense YOUR presence

Date:_____

_____

_____

_____

_____

_____

_____

_____

_____

_____

_____

_____

_____

_____

_____

_____

In His Chambers

Joshua 1:5-6a (ICB)

Just as I was with Moses, so I will be with you. No one will be able to stop you all your life. I will not leave you. I will never leave you alone. "Joshua, be strong and brave!"

Help me to know that I do not need to understand why something is happening as much as I need to know that YOU are with me...

Open the eyes understanding

Date:_____

_____
_____
_____
_____
_____
_____
_____
_____
_____
_____
_____
_____
_____
_____
_____

In His Chambers

Genesis 39:1-2 (ICB)

Now Joseph had been taken down to Egypt. An Egyptian named Potiphar was an officer to the king of Egypt. He was the captain of the palace guard. He bought Joseph from the Ishmaelites who had brought him down there. The Lord was with Joseph, and he became a successful man.

Help my faith to remain strong...

Jesus, please pray for me

Date:_____

_____

_____

_____

_____

_____

_____

_____

_____

_____

_____

_____

_____

_____

_____

In His Chambers

1 Peter 1:6-8 (TLB)

So be truly glad! There is wonderful joy ahead, even though the going is rough for a while down here. These trials are only to test your faith, to see whether or not it is strong and pure. It is being tested as fire tests gold and purifies it—and your faith is far more precious to God than mere gold; so if your faith remains strong after being tried in the test tube of fiery trials, it will bring you much praise and glory and honor...

Many there be which say of my soul, there is no help for him in God. Selah. But thou, O Lord, art a shield for me; my glory, and the lifter up of mine head...

Psalm 3:2-3 (KJV)

Date:_____

Help! I am speaking but not so sure I am praying...
I am going to be quiet now so I can hear YOU speak

Date:_____

_____

_____

_____

_____

_____

_____

_____

_____

_____

_____

_____

In His Chambers

I Samuel 1:2-20(NKJV)

...Hannah had no children... And she was in bitterness of soul, and prayed unto the Lord, and wept sore. Now Hannah, she spake in her heart; only her lips moved, but her voice was not heard: therefore Eli thought she had been drunk... Hannah answered and said, No, my lord, I am a woman of a sorrowful spirit... Then Eli answered and said, Go in peace: and the God of Israel grant thee thy petition... Hannah had conceived, that she bare a son, and called his name Samuel...

Lord YOUR presence is our Help...
Guide us with YOUR eyes

Date:_____

_____

_____

_____

_____

_____

_____

_____

_____

_____

_____

_____

_____

_____

_____

_____

_____

In His Chambers

II Chronicles 20:16-17 (NLT)

Tomorrow, march out against them. You will find them coming up through the ascent of Ziz at the end of the valley that opens into the wilderness of Jeruel. But you will not even need to fight. Take your positions; then stand still and watch the Lord's victory. He is with you, O people of Judah and Jerusalem. Do not be afraid or discouraged. Go out against them tomorrow, for the Lord is with you!

Lord, thank YOU for sending help!

Write a thank you letter to someone (a spouse, friend, parent, neighbor, sibling, stranger, teacher, minister, bank teller...) that you know God sent your way to help you. If you can, give the letter to that person: it will be refreshingly encouraging to them.

Date:_____

_____

_____

_____

_____

_____

_____

_____

_____

_____

_____

_____

_____

_____

_____

_____

_____

_____

_____

Worth the Journey

It is always worth the journey with YOU
YOU always make sure what YOU bring me to, YOU see me through
No matter how much turbulence in the beginning I see
Somehow YOU always manage to make the end worth it for me
I see random ingredients all tossed in the pot of my life
But you see the perfect soup to serve to others who are hungry for Christ

It is always worth the sacrifice with YOU
Whether I am delaying gratitude or giving up what I desire to hold on to
No matter how thirsty I am for acceptance, peace, joy, love or to succeed
My best experiences are when I say "Yes LORD" & "YOU lead"
Sacrifices are works of faith that impregnate the ground of today's reality
So I can harvest the amazing future that God has placed inside of me

It is always worth choosing YOU as my priority
I am always amazed at the outcomes when I follow YOUR authority
If I am lead to the palace or to the crucifixion scene of my destiny
I trust that all is working to fulfill the good plans YOU have for me
When the SPIRIT speaks, it is with God's love and in God's Devine will
So I'll move when HE says and I'll stop when HE says my child be still

Everything, every road, every experience, every loss,
every relationship, every sickness, every set back, every come
up, every burial, every resurrection and every moment of my
life is worth the journey - as long as the I AM is with me…

Prayer: Lord help me to confidently remember that today's
correction, sacrifice and reprioritization does not compare
to the Glory my life will embrace tomorrow.

Call to Me, and I will answer you. I will tell you of great things, things beyond
what you can imagine, things you could never have known.
                                                    Jerimiah 3:33 (VOICE)

Help me navigate through this_____

(Fill in the blank: divorce, disappointment, sickness, discouragement, offense, promotion, breakthrough, reconciliation…)

I will trust the Lord's instructions!

Date:_____

_____

_____

_____

_____

_____

_____

_____

_____

_____

_____

_____

_____

_____

_____

_____

In His Chambers

Proverbs 3:5-7b (NLT)

Trust in the Lord with all your heart; do not depend on your own understanding. Seek his will in all you do, and he will show you which path to take. Do not be impressed with your own wisdom.

Help me to know that Jesus loves me...

and that nothing can separate us from HIS love

Date:_____

_____

_____

_____

_____

_____

_____

_____

_____

_____

_____

_____

_____

_____

_____

_____

In His Chambers

Romans 8:38-39 (KJV)

For I am persuaded, that neither death, nor life, nor angels, nor principalities, nor powers, nor things present, nor things to come, nor height, nor depth, nor any other creature, shall be able to separate us from the love of God, which is in Christ Jesus our Lord.

Why Journal? *(page 1 of 2)*

Journal so that you can remember, the good plans God has for you
So that you will not forget all HE brought you to and through
Journal to remember who God is and the promises HE has made
So that you will believe HIS report – especially when answers are delayed
Journal to keep your hope anchored and your faith alive
Journal until you do not believe the enemy's threats and lies
Journal so that your tongue does not deny God in times of uncertainty
Especially when you hear the taunting heavy footsteps of adversity
Journal the lyrics of scriptures to sing as you followed Jehovah out
Out of seasons of loss, wilderness, darkness, sickness and drought
Journal the times God refreshed you with blessings from unexpected places
And how God so lovingly robed you in the apparel of HIS everlasting graces
Journal to archive the characteristics of God that you have already learned
So that when your faith is tried, it will have a point of reference that is firm
Journal to spray paint the Word of God on the walls of your heart
Journal so you can believe to see the expected end before the trial starts
Journal to give voice to silent dreams and to silence the voice of hesitation
Journal the order of the steps you must take to experience restoration
Journal to write autobiographies of your testimonies and answers to your prayers
Share them with others so they will know that God is listening and HE cares
Journal to remember the people and moments that are simply priceless
Like family, friends and that moment when God's forgiveness left you breathless
Like birthdays, beach days and hope-filled days
And my favorite: I am better than my yesterdays

Journal to remember the day Jesus moved into your heart to stay
And the tears you shed the instant you realized that Jesus is the only way
Journal what you want to see in your tomorrow
Journal to create a grave yard for unwanted bitterness and sorrow
Journal to stop the spread of vile words whose only mission is to hurt
Journal a love note to God for HIS healing and HIS mighty works
Journal to recall that God does miracles when your answer tank is at zero
Journal so that it is well known that God alone is your number one Hero
Journal to experience harvest before it comes
And to meditate on all that Jesus has done
Journal God's Word so that your faith will acquire a taste for HIS goodness
Journal to create a road sign for God's realities and to trust in GOD's holiness
Journal your love for God and give HIM glory, honor, praise and adoration
Journal to give thanks to HIM not "for every" but "in every" situation
Journal your prayers no matter how great or how small
So when you read your journal later, you will be amazed at how God answered them all

Journal, Journal, Journal and Journal some more!

Now all praise to God for his wonderful kindness to us and his favor that he has poured out upon us because we belong to his dearly loved Son. So overflowing is his kindness toward us that he took away all our sins through the blood of his Son, by whom we are saved...

Ephesians 1:6-7 (TLB)

Date:_____

_____

_____

_____

_____

_____

_____

_____

_____

_____

_____

_____

_____

_____

_____

_____

_____

_____

_____

_____

In His Chambers

Help me go home...
I have been prodigal and away from "the family" long enough

Date:_____

_____

_____

_____

_____

_____

_____

_____

_____

_____

_____

_____

_____

_____

_____

_____

_____

_____

_____

_____

In His Chambers

Luke 15:17-20 (KJV)

And when he came to himself, he said...I will arise and go to my father, and will say unto him, Father, I have sinned against heaven, and before thee...And he arose, and came to his father. But when he was yet a great way off, his father saw him, and had compassion, and ran, and fell on his neck, and kissed him.

Help my love for YOU be my cause to live for YOU...

because YOUR love was cause enough to die for me

Date:_____

_____

_____

_____

_____

_____

_____

_____

_____

_____

_____

_____

_____

_____

_____

_____

_____

_____

_____

In His Chambers

Galatians 5:13-14 (NLT)

For you have been called to live in freedom, my brothers and sisters. But do not use your freedom to satisfy your sinful nature. Instead, use your freedom to serve one another in love. For the whole law can be summed up in this one command: "Love your neighbor as yourself."

Help me to give to ministries that spread the gospel...

with the joy in knowing that I am giving others the gift to know God's Love through JESUS

Date:_____

_____
_____
_____
_____
_____
_____
_____
_____
_____
_____
_____
_____
_____
_____
_____
_____

In His Chambers

Mathew 6:32-33 (KJV)

(For after all these things do the Gentiles seek:) for your heavenly Father knoweth that ye have need of all these things. But seek ye first the kingdom of God, and his righteousness; and all these things shall be added unto you.

My eyes are always looking to the Lord for help. He will keep me from any traps...

Psalm 25:15 (ICB)

Date:_____

_____

_____

_____

_____

_____

_____

_____

_____

_____

_____

_____

_____

_____

_____

_____

_____

_____

_____

_____

_____

_____

_____

Help me know that there is but one way for my sins to be forgiven and my soul to be saved...
Jesus is the way to salvation and the forgiveness of sin

Date:_____

_____

_____

_____

_____

_____

_____

_____

_____

_____

_____

_____

_____

_____

_____

In His Chambers

Mathew 1:21 (KJV)

And she shall bring forth a son, and thou shalt call his name Jesus: for he shall save his people from their sins.

Romans 10:9 (NIV)

If you declare with your mouth, "Jesus is Lord," and believe in your heart that God raised him from the dead, you will be saved.

Help! I need YOUR grace...
to empower me to keep on saying yes to YOUR ways

Date:_____

_____

_____

_____

_____

_____

_____

_____

_____

_____

_____

_____

_____

_____

_____

_____

_____

_____

_____

_____

In His Chambers

1 Corinthians 1:7 (TLB)

Now you have every grace and blessing; every spiritual gift and power for doing his will are yours during this time of waiting for the return of our Lord Jesus Christ...

Therefore he is able to save completely those who come to God through him (Jesus), because he always lives to intercede for them. Such a high priest truly meets our need—one who is holy, blameless, pure, set apart from sinners, exalted above the heavens...

Hebrews 7:25-26 (NIV)

Date:_____

_____

_____

_____

_____

_____

_____

_____

_____

_____

_____

_____

_____

_____

_____

_____

_____

_____

In His Chambers

Help me avoid putting on shame, guilt and regret...
and accept God's remedy for sin: salvation then forgetfulness

Date:_____

_____

_____

_____

_____

_____

_____

_____

_____

_____

_____

_____

_____

_____

_____

_____

_____

In His Chambers

Hebrews 8:12 (TLB)

And I will be merciful to them in their wrongdoings, and I will remember their sins no more."

With joy you will draw water from the wells of salvation...

Isaiah 12:3 (NIV)

Date:_____

_____

_____

_____

_____

_____

_____

_____

_____

_____

_____

_____

_____

_____

_____

_____

_____

_____

_____

_____

_____

_____

I have a right to smile
After all, I have a Savior who walked the "Green Mile"
Not for crimes that HE had done
Nor because He drew the short straw and won
But because Jesus desired all men to be in God's family
To walk in heavenly places and to do life abundantly

So I will Smile
Smile because I am an heir
And because God Almighty was, is and will always be there
To father me, defend me, teach me, strengthen me
To forgive me, mold me and graciously love on me

I will Smile
Smile without hesitation
Every time I ponder the "Passion of Christ" and
and the price HE paid for our salvation
When I think about where HE brought me from
And where HE is taking me to
A gratitude smile seems so little to offer for all YOU do
My smile is not without a cause
My smile is my praise and my applause

So I will Smile
Smile because God called me the apple of HIS eye
HE sings over me! He hears my every cry!
HE gave me his name and with it such wealth
HE gave me joy unspeakable and peace filled health

My Smile was brought with the prefect LAMB's blood
so I could experience authentic complete Love
Oh Yes! You have a right to smile

So **Smile**

He forgives your sins—every one. He heals

your diseases— every one. He redeems

you from hell—saves your life! He crowns

you with love and mercy—a paradise

crown. He wraps you in goodness—

beauty eternal. He renews your youth—

you're always young in his presence.

Psalm 103:3-5 (MSG)

Help me see the truth about Jesus...

Holy Spirit reveal Him and I will believe Him

Date:_____

_____

_____

_____

_____

_____

_____

_____

_____

_____

_____

_____

_____

_____

_____

In His Chambers

Matthew 16:15-17 (NLT)

Then he asked them, "But who do you say I am?" Simon Peter answered, "You are the Messiah, the Son of the living God." Jesus replied, "You are blessed, Simon son of John, because my Father in heaven has revealed this to you. You did not learn this from any human being...

Help me spread the good news of the gospel...
So others will know Jesus and that HE IS BEAUTIFUL

Date:_____

_____

_____

_____

_____

_____

_____

_____

_____

_____

_____

_____

_____

In His Chambers

2 Corinthians 5:17-19 (TLB)

When someone becomes a Christian, he becomes a brand new person inside... All these new things are from God who brought us back to himself through what Christ Jesus did. And God has given us the privilege of urging everyone to come into his favor and be reconciled to him...no longer counting men's sins against them but blotting them out. This is the wonderful message he has given us to tell others.

Jesus replied, "What I am telling you so earnestly is this: Unless one is born of water and the Spirit, he cannot enter the Kingdom of God. Men can only reproduce human life, but the Holy Spirit gives new life from heaven; so do not be surprised at my statement that you must be born again!..."

John 3:5-7 (TLB)

Date:_____

_____

_____

_____

_____

_____

_____

_____

_____

_____

_____

_____

_____

_____

_____

_____

_____

_____

_____

_____

I have written this to you who believe in the Son of God so that you may know you have eternal life. And we are sure of this, that he will listen to us whenever we ask him for anything in line with his will. And if we really know he is listening when we talk to him and make our requests, then we can be sure that he will answer us...

1 John 5:13-15 (TLB)

Date:_____

Lord, Thank YOU for
sending Jesus!

Write at least 10 statements that begin with "Jesus thank you for helping_____."

For example: Jesus thank you for helping me forgive my spouse for cheating on me; Jesus thank you for helping this business be profitable; Jesus thank you for helping by stopping that car from hitting us; Jesus thank you for helping me be healed from sickness and the darkness of grief...

    WE HAVE SO MUCH TO THANK JESUS FOR!

Date:_____

_____

_____

_____

_____

_____

_____

_____

_____

_____

_____

_____

_____

_____

_____

_____

_____

_____

_____

Help me remain in love with my first love...

God the Father
God the Son
God the Holy Spirit

Date:_____

_____

_____

_____

_____

_____

_____

_____

_____

_____

_____

_____

_____

In His Chambers

I John 4:18-21 (KJV)

There is no fear in love; but perfect love casteth out fear: because fear hath torment. He that feareth is not made perfect in love. We love him, because he first loved us. If a man say, I love God, and hateth his brother, he is a liar: for he that loveth not his brother whom he hath seen, how can he love God whom he hath not seen? And this commandment have we from him, That he who loveth God love his brother also.

Help me to lean on YOU...
not riches
not authorities
not worldly wisdom

Date:_____

_____

_____

_____

_____

_____

_____

_____

_____

_____

_____

_____

_____

_____

_____

_____

In His Chambers

Psalm 20:6-8 (TLB)

"God save the king"—I know he does! He hears me from highest heaven and sends great victories. Some nations boast of armies and of weaponry, but our boast is in the Lord our God. Those nations will collapse and perish; we will arise to stand firm and sure!

As for me, since I am poor and needy, let the Lord keep me in his thoughts. You are my helper and my savior. O my God, do not delay.

Psalm 40:17 (NLT)

Date:_____

_____

_____

_____

_____

_____

_____

_____

_____

_____

_____

_____

_____

_____

_____

_____

_____

_____

_____

_____

_____

_____

I laid me down and slept; I awaked; for the Lord sustained me...

Psalm 3:5 (KJV)

Date:_____

_____

_____

_____

_____

_____

_____

_____

_____

_____

_____

_____

_____

_____

_____

_____

_____

_____

_____

When doctors are saying "I will never" and others are saying "I cannot", Help me...
to keep saying "I believe" the report of the Lord

Date:_____

_____

_____

_____

_____

_____

_____

_____

_____

_____

_____

_____

_____

_____

In His Chambers

Mathew 9:19-21 (ICB)

And so Jesus stood up and went with the ruler. Jesus' followers went too. Then a woman who had been bleeding for 12 years came behind Jesus and touched the edge of his coat. She was thinking, "If I can touch his coat, then I will be healed."

READ ME MY RIGHTS: Life

I have a right to ask for Life, after all Jesus died for me
I have a right to declare "Life"
So I will
Pray for Life
Envision Life
Expect Life
I will
Seek the Creator of Life
For steps of Life
I will follow the
Good Shepherd of Life
Out of the valley and shadows of death
I have a right to ask for Life
After all, Jesus' nail scared hands
purchased my Life
So I will
Pursue Life
Apprehend Life
Rest in Life
And abundantly live Life
Life in my Body, Mind and Spirit
Life in my Vision, Purpose and Joy
Life in my Ministry, Relationships and Love
Everywhere the weapon of death seeks to prosper
I will speak and seek Life
Life in Christ
Oh Yes! You have a right to Life!
After all Jesus died for you

*So **Live!***

...I am come that they might have life, and that they might have
it more abundantly John 10:10 (KJV)

Listen to my prayer, O God, do not ignore my plea...
Psalm 55:1 (NIV)

Date:_____

_____

_____

_____

_____

_____

_____

_____

_____

_____

_____

_____

_____

_____

_____

_____

_____

_____

_____

_____

_____

_____

_____

_____

Help me to know that my emptiness...

is the ideal condition for YOU to fill me with love, power and a sound mind

Date:_____

_____

_____

_____

_____

_____

_____

_____

_____

_____

_____

_____

_____

_____

_____

_____

_____

_____

_____

In His Chambers

Luke 1:53a (ICB)

God fills the hungry with good things...

Lord help mend my broken heart...

because I want to experience loving YOU with all my heart

Date:_____

_____
_____
_____
_____
_____
_____
_____
_____
_____
_____
_____
_____
_____
_____
_____
_____
_____
_____
_____

In His Chambers

Psalm 147:3 (ICB)

He heals the brokenhearted. He bandages their wounds.

Help! I am grieving...
comfort me Holy Spirit with the TRUTH that is in Christ Jesus

Date:_____

_____
_____
_____
_____
_____
_____
_____
_____
_____
_____
_____
_____
_____
_____
_____
_____
_____

In His Chambers

2 Corinthians 1:3-4 (TLB)

What a wonderful God we have—he is the Father of our Lord Jesus Christ, the source of every mercy, and the one who so wonderfully comforts and strengthens us in our hardships and trials. And why does he do this? So that when others are troubled, needing our sympathy and encouragement, we can pass on to them this same help and comfort God has given us.

Until Morning Comes (page 1 of 2)

Father,
This has left me speechless and I do not know what to pray nor what to think, want, need or even what to feel. I find it difficult to open my mouth with words of hope.

Jesus,
I must rely on your perfect love to instruct the Holy Spirit to take these tears and translate them into words: words of honor, praise, thanksgiving and supplication. My muffled thoughts, mewling and groans are surface expressions of the pain, disappointment, famine and faintness that I feel.

Holy Spirit,
I know that you are fluent in the language of tears, moans, silent screams, weariness and fatigue. Tonight, not by my prayers but by YOUR prayers' alone, I and my family will find a response and rest.

Lord,
Thanks for handling the flow of my tears like droplets of I grade, round brilliant cut, three carat, priceless diamonds. The current of YOUR comfort is pushing through my tears, cleansing my focus and unveiling the compassion and greatness of YOUR love.

Until Morning Comes

I can feel the breath of YOUR presence resuscitating my strength, body, mind and YOUR hymns of praise. Even now, as I **"STOP and PRAY",** the voice of YOUR scriptures are singing over the countenance of my soul. YOUR song is preserving me and commanding my circumstances.

Peace! Stand still and do not move from her mind!
Hope! Anchor yourself on the ROCK of her salvation!
Health! Cease your unsteadiness and grip firmly to her body!
Blessings! Come out from your hiding and overtake her!
These are the lyrics that God Almighty sings over me.
GOD fights for my Survival and Healing! And so will I.
GOD fights for His Glory and Honor! And so will I.
HE fights and HE always wins! And so will I.

Today's tears will be tomorrow's testimonies of God's amazing grace, HIS unfailing strength, HIS plenteous mercies, HIS accomplishing Word, HIS miraculous power, HIS everlasting love and HIS guiding light of fire preserving us Until Morning Comes.

**...weeping may endure for a night,
but joy cometh in the morning.**
(Psalm 30:5b KJV)

Then he turned my sorrow into joy! He took away my clothes of mourning and clothed me with joy...

Psalm 30:11 (TLB)

Date:_____

_____

_____

_____

_____

_____

_____

_____

_____

_____

_____

_____

_____

_____

_____

_____

_____

_____

_____

_____

_____

_____

Jesus help me to remember YOU in times of crisis...
just like YOU remembered me in the garden of Gethsemane

Date:_____

_____

_____

_____

_____

_____

_____

_____

_____

_____

_____

_____

_____

_____

_____

_____

_____

In His Chambers

Mathew 26:39 (ICB)

Then Jesus walked a little farther away from them. He fell to the ground and prayed, "My Father, if it is possible, do not give me this cup of suffering. But do what you want, not what I want.

Help, I want to be healed...
Lord Jesus, touch me or
I will touch YOU

Date:_____

_____

_____

_____

_____

_____

_____

_____

_____

_____

_____

_____

_____

_____

_____

_____

_____

_____

_____

In His Chambers

Luke 8:43-46 (ICB)

A woman was there who had been bleeding for 12 years. She had spent all her money on doctors...The woman came up behind Jesus and touched the edge of his coat. At that moment, her bleeding stopped. Then Jesus said, "Who touched me?"..."Someone did touch me! I felt power go out from me."

See, God has come to save me! I will trust and not be afraid, for the Lord is my strength and song; he is my salvation...

Isaiah 12:2 (TLB)

Date:_____

_____
_____
_____
_____
_____
_____
_____
_____
_____
_____
_____
_____
_____
_____
_____
_____
_____
_____
_____

Unexpected Help!

Have you ever dreamed to experience something in your life, only to have the extraordinary fortune of birthing that dream but the misfortune of not seeing it mature? You had the fertility to birth the marriage, but the end was divorce; you started the business but what once read articles of incorporation, now reads bankruptcy; you did the hard work to become a first- generation college student and now you are a first-generation college dropout; you faithfully contributed to your 401K but unfortunately not to your retirement. There are times when our choices disease the maturation of our dreams, but then, there are other times when the winds of life capsizes them and our dreams become the tragedy of a perfectly executed crocodile death roll. Leaving only the remains of the dream to be processioned into the overcrowded Bag & Tag Dream Cemetery. I have had such a dream, have you?

*My dream, it was finely dressed for burial: a custom tailored suit designed by **Too Many Excuses Limited**. A **This Should Have Been Mine** silk tie with matching pocket square purchased from **Fear Designs.com**. Cambridge Italian leather slip on dress shoes shipped in by **I Don' t Need Any Help Corporation.** Hollywood Sky Blue socks by **Tragedy LLC** and an exquisite timepiece engineered by **Fault My Past Luxury Jewelers**. Via Dolorosa mourners dressing me with loose fitting words of comfort: "there will be other dreams", "try again later", "God works in mysterious ways" and "well at least you birthed the dream and watched it grow a little - that was more than what I did." However, I wanted my dream to have more time, more seasons, more opportunities, more impact and more influence; I thought there would be more! just more! I wanted the dream to extend pass my garage and into the world. But, all the votes were in. I had done all I could do and so, with tears, I conceded to death's crocodile roll.*

Unexpected Help!

BUT! LIFE, HIMSELF, was on the same road that shaped the footsteps of the pallbearers that held my precious, precious dream. Jesus heard my tears, had compassion, and touched the casket with HIS resurrection power (Selah). Oh! The joy that flooded my soul † and the gratitude that rained from my lips † the gaze of appreciation from my eyes was like the eyes of a baby focused on his mother while breast-feeding † Oh! The hope that pulse through the veins of my heart † and the loyalty that overflowed for such loving kindness † All of this delightful wonder was mine because of the compassion of Christ. HE subdued the opportunity to extend HIS unexpected help. Not just any kind of help but GOD level help!

Unexpected light in a season of grief and darkness. Unexpected shelter in a time of a storm. An unexpected breakthrough where a wall once stood. An unexpected adversary to my adversary. An unexpected allied warrior King after I had walked away from the battle. An unexpected deliver after 38 years of addiction. Unexpected strength while the referee was midway through the count. An unexpected healing after the family met with the doctor. An unexpected refuge in the time of a pandemic.

Unexpected help yields unexpected testimonies about the greatness of God. Today it was my dream but tomorrow it could be your marriage, business, health, womb, ministry, mind or your child that starts living, producing, evolving and bearing fruit because of the Lord's unexpected help.

Jesus is a resurrectionist
Jesus is the Resurrection

Unexpected Help!

Jesus is the Bread of Life
Jesus is Life

Luke 7:11-17(TLB)

Not long afterwards, Jesus went with his disciples to the village of Nain... A funeral procession was coming out as he approached the village gate. The boy who had died was the only son of his widowed mother, and many mourners from the village were with her. When the Lord saw her, his heart overflowed with sympathy. "Do not cry!" he said. Then he walked over to the coffin and touched it, and the bearers stopped. "Laddie," he said, "come back to life again." Then the boy sat up and began to talk to those around him! And Jesus gave him back to his mother. A great fear swept the crowd, and they exclaimed with praises to God, "A mighty prophet has risen among us," and, "We have seen the hand of God at work today." The report of what he did that day raced from end to end of Judea and even out across the borders.

THANK YOU, LORD JESUS, FOR BEING OUR UNEXPECTED HELP!

Prayer: Holy Spirit help us to walk in the image of JESUS and be unexpected help to others!

Lord help me remember that YOU are faithful and I can trust YOU to supply all I need, even when all I need... is to believe YOUR Word!

My confidence and hope
is in the integrity of
the God of the
scriptures!

Date:_____

_____

_____

_____

_____

_____

_____

_____

_____

_____

_____

_____

_____

In His Chambers

Hebrews 10:35-36 (ICB)

So do not lose the courage that you had in the past. It has a great reward. You must hold on, so you can do what God wants and receive what he has promised.

Help, the land of my faith is in a famine...

because my hope has parked
in a dry and fruitless place
and I lack the strength to relocate

Date:_____

_____
_____
_____
_____
_____
_____
_____
_____
_____
_____
_____
_____
_____
_____
_____

In His Chambers

Isaiah 41:17-18 (KJV)

When the poor and needy seek water, and there is none, and their tongue faileth for thirst, I the Lord will hear them, I the God of Israel will not forsake them. I will open rivers in high places, and fountains in the midst of the valleys: I will make the wilderness a pool of water, and the dry land springs of water.

Lord help me hide from my enemies...

so I can catch my breath

Date:_____

_____
_____
_____
_____
_____
_____
_____
_____
_____
_____
_____
_____
_____
_____
_____
_____
_____
_____
_____

In His Chambers

Psalm 46:1(NLT)

God is our refuge and strength, always ready to help in times of trouble.

The Lord will keep you from all harm—he will watch over your life; the Lord will watch over your coming and going both now and forevermore...

Psalm 121:7-8 (NIV)

Date:_____

_____
_____
_____
_____
_____
_____
_____
_____
_____
_____
_____
_____
_____
_____
_____
_____
_____
_____
_____

In His Chambers

Help I am struggling to praise YOU in this moment...

my faith will sing: YOU are GOD and YOU are GOOD

Date:_____

_____

_____

_____

_____

_____

_____

_____

_____

_____

_____

_____

_____

_____

_____

_____

In His Chambers

Psalm 28:7 (KJV)

The Lord is my strength and my shield; my heart trusted in him, and I am helped: therefore my heart greatly rejoiceth; and with my song will I praise him.

Help me cry out...
for Jesus, to Jesus and the name Jesus

Date:_____

_____

_____

_____

_____

_____

_____

_____

_____

_____

_____

_____

_____

_____

_____

_____

_____

_____

_____

_____

_____

In His Chambers

Psalm 31:22 (NLT)

In panic I cried out, "I am cut off from the Lord!" But you heard my cry for mercy and answered my call for help.

In my desperation, I prayed, and the Lord listened; he saved me from all my troubles. For the angel of the Lord is a guard; he surrounds and defends all who fear him. Taste and see that the Lord is good. Oh, the joys of those who take refuge in him!

Psalm 34:6-8 (NLT)

Date:_____

_____

_____

_____

_____

_____

_____

_____

_____

_____

_____

_____

_____

_____

_____

_____

_____

_____

_____

In His Chambers

Help I'm Sinking

Do not get me wrong
I did not start out like this.
When I started, my steps were sure,
large and in charge, full of faith.
My bodacious confidence was
attractive.
No storm could stop me!
No wind could wobble me!
Every step ordered - was a step taken.
Like a decorated soldier, I marched by
the thoughts of my Commander and
Chief.
No fear!
No doubt!
I was walking by faith in the impossible,
because I had heard the only answer
that matters when impossible ask:
Can I do that? Can I do what I see?

I see **WOMEN** preachers, CEOs,
professors, prime ministers, ballers,
entomologist, presidents and much
more.
I see activists, warriors, game
changers, authors, scientist, and cyber
entrepreneurs.
I see women rocking these roles with
tailored apparel of confidence, humility,
intellect and poise.

Can I do that? Can I do what I see?

I see **MEN** of superior commitment,
work ethic, compassion and loyalty.
Living their lives devoted to the
betterment of their homes and the global
family.
I see generational success, influence,
leadership and prosperity.
I see men whose first defense and
reason for living concreted in charity.

Do not get me wrong
I was doing the impossible, because I
heard the only answer that matters when
Divinity is ask:
Can I do that? Can I do what I see?

I see **SONS** no longer abused by the
hand of poverty,
but mentored by hands of purpose and
destiny.
I see sons being keepers of their
brothers,
living as servant-kings yet still honoring
their fathers and mothers.
I see sons as entrepreneurs not derailed
by the tongues that lack knowledge.
Sons achieving dreams of turning
tassels on Tudor bonnets in college.

Can I do that? Can I do what I see?

Help I'm Sinking

I see **DAUGHTERS** not trafficked by war and greed,
but slaves only to God's divine good will, good plans and fruitful deeds.
I see daughters dancing to drum beats of doctors, engineers, bishops, sisterhood, directors and such.
I see daughters respecting themselves and giving Much Love and Loving Much.

Do not get me wrong
I did not start out like this.
When I started, my steps were sure, large and in charge, full of faith. My bodacious confidence was attractive.
I heard the only answer that matters when Greatness is asked:
Can I do that? Can I do what I see?

The answer was COME! COME be what you SEE!

I was walking in the impossible!
Strutting pass generational curses!
Leaping out of emotional prisons!
Unmoved by the winds of insecurity, lack and adversity.
Living in the impossible, just like I saw!
I was achieving my purpose and answering the call.

I was walking on WORD in water!
Just Like Jesus!
I am not sure if it was the image of my pride or my fear.
That drew my attention to the wind and waves that were near.
The neck of my focus turned and I defaulted into crisis thinking.
In a panic, I tossed over the cargo of my faith and started sinking.
I cried for hope & help! And Jesus did the only thing that matters when a cry is heard:

**HE REACHED OUT HIS
HAND and HELPED.**

So if you see a woman's garment of confidence mauled by fists and words of violence,
or a man's grief consuming him as he suffers in silence,
or a daughter's self-worth enslaved by the need for others acceptance and praise,
or a son's dreams deformed by too many fatherless nights and smoked filled days:
Do not just look at me, us or them and say: what in the world were they thinking!
I plead with you, be the hand of Christ and reach out while you can still hear:
"Help me I'm sinking!"

Help! I am sinking...
reach for me Jesus!

Date:_____

_____

_____

_____

_____

_____

_____

_____

_____

_____

_____

_____

_____

_____

_____

_____

_____

_____

_____

_____

_____

_____

In His Chambers

Mathew 14:30 (KJV)

But when he saw the wind boisterous, he was afraid; and beginning to sink, he cried, saying, Lord, save me.

Help! I am in a dark place...
Lord Jesus, this sin is blinding me
I surrender to YOUR truth and leading

Date:_____

_____

_____

_____

_____

_____

_____

_____

_____

_____

_____

_____

_____

_____

_____

_____

_____

_____

_____

In His Chambers

John 8:12 (NLT)

Jesus spoke to the people once more and said, "I am the light of the world. If you follow me, you won't have to walk in darkness, because you will have the light that leads to life."

Help I need assembling...
I think I have all the parts but
I am not quite put together

Date:_____

_____

_____

_____

_____

_____

_____

_____

_____

_____

_____

_____

_____

_____

_____

_____

_____

In His Chambers

Ezekiel 37:3-5, 14a (KJV)

...The Lord said to me, "Prophesy to these bones. Say to them, 'Dry bones, hear the word of the Lord. This is what the Lord God says to the bones: I will cause breath to enter you. Then you will live. I will put muscles on you. I will put flesh on you. I will cover you with skin. Then I will put breath in you, and you will live. Then you will know that I am the Lord.'"

Help, I have stopped crying, but I am still hurting...
I need YOUR healing and comfort

Date:_____

_____

_____

_____

_____

_____

_____

_____

_____

_____

_____

_____

_____

_____

_____

_____

_____

_____

In His Chambers

Psalm 34:18 (NLV)

The Lord is close to the brokenhearted; he rescues those whose spirits are crushed.

Help me not to carry burdens that are meant to be casted away...
into YOUR more than capable hands

Date:_____

_____
_____
_____
_____
_____
_____
_____
_____
_____
_____
_____
_____
_____
_____
_____
_____
_____
_____

In His Chambers

Psalm 55:22 (TLB)

Give your burdens to the Lord. He will carry them. He will not permit the godly to slip or fall.

Our help is in the name of the Lord, the Maker of heaven and earth

Psalm 124:8 (NIV)

Date:_____

In His Chambers

Help, the Liar (Satan) is planting thoughts of suicide...

This is how much God loved
the world: He gave his Son
his one and only Son. And this is why:
so that no one need be destroyed;
by believing in him, anyone
can have a whole and lasting life
John 3:16-17 MSG

Date:_____

_____

_____

_____

_____

_____

_____

GOD IS STILL WRITING
YOUR STORY

In His Chambers

1-800-525-5683	K-Love Prayer Line
1-800-273-8255	National Suicide Prevention Lifeline
Dial 988	24 hour Suicide and Crisis Lifeline
Visit website	www.betterhelp.com

Help me Lord to know that YOU knew me then and YOU know me now...
and YOU have a purpose and good plan for every day of my life

Date:_____

_____

_____

_____

_____

_____

_____

_____

_____

_____

_____

_____

_____

_____

_____

_____

_____

In His Chambers

Jeremiah 1:5a (ICB)

Before I made you in your mother's womb, I chose you. Before you were born, I set you apart for a special work.

But the Lord says, "I will now rise up because the poor are being hurt. Because of the moans of the helpless, I will give them the help they want."

Psalm 12:5 (ICB)

Date:_____

Help, I feel so inadequate...
but LORD YOU are all
sufficient and ALMIGHTY!

Date:_____

_____

_____

_____

_____

_____

_____

_____

_____

_____

_____

_____

_____

_____

_____

_____

_____

_____

_____

In His Chambers

2 Chronicles 14:11 (ICB)

Asa called out to the Lord his God. He said, "Lord, only you can help weak people against the strong. Help us, Lord our God. We depend on you. We fight against this large army in your name. Lord, you are our God. Do not let anyone win against you."

Help, I need freedom from this turbulence...

the winds of life are blowing me apart - I need YOUR peace to hold me together

Date:_____

_____

_____

_____

_____

_____

_____

_____

_____

_____

_____

In His Chambers

Psalm 83:1 (KJV)

Keep not thou silence, O God: hold not thy peace, and be not still, O God.

Mark 4:37-39 (NLT)

...a fierce storm came up. High waves were breaking into the boat, and it began to fill with water. Jesus was sleeping at the back of the boat...The disciples woke him up, shouting, "Teacher, do not you care that we're going to drown?"...he rebuked the wind and said to the waves, "Silence! Be still!" Suddenly the wind stopped, and there was a great calm.

Help! "This" is too heavy...
Catch Jesus! I am hurling
"This" YOUR way

Date:_____

_____

_____

_____

_____

_____

_____

_____

_____

_____

_____

_____

_____

_____

_____

_____

_____

_____

_____

_____

_____

In His Chambers

I Peter 5:7 (KJV)

Casting all your care upon him; for he careth for you.

But as for me, I am poor and needy; please hurry to my aid, O God. You are my helper and my savior; O Lord, do not delay.

Psalm 70:5 (NLT)

Date:_____

_____

_____

_____

_____

_____

_____

_____

_____

_____

_____

_____

_____

_____

_____

_____

_____

_____

_____

_____

_____

_____

Lord send Help! I am sinking...
YOUR blessing is weighing down my boat

Date:_____

_____
_____
_____
_____
_____
_____
_____
_____
_____
_____
_____
_____
_____
_____
_____
_____

In His Chambers

Luke 5:7 (TLB)

A shout for help brought their partners in the other boat, and soon both boats were filled with fish and on the verge of sinking.

Lord, many thanks to YOU for helping!!!

Write a thank you note to Jesus for being a present help at a time when you were in trouble.

Date:_____

_____

_____

_____

_____

_____

_____

_____

_____

_____

_____

_____

_____

_____

_____

_____

_____

_____

_____

_____

_____

Distress I screamed to the Lord for his help. And he heard me from heaven; my cry reached his ears...
Psalm 18:6 (TLB)

Date:_____

_____
_____
_____
_____
_____
_____
_____
_____
_____
_____
_____
_____
_____
_____
_____
_____
_____
_____
_____
_____
_____
_____
_____
_____

Help! I am unemployed and scared...

God knows
God cares
God will provide

Date:_____

_____
_____
_____
_____
_____
_____
_____
_____
_____
_____
_____
_____
_____
_____

In His Chambers

Isaiah 41:10 (NLT)

Do not be afraid, for I am with you. Do not be discouraged, for I am your God. I will strengthen you and help you. I will hold you up with my victorious right hand.

"Daddy I can't reach it!" was the declaration of Hannah. The three year old, who had somehow managed to kneel her way up the steps that lead to the Bankers Museum Park playground slide. Hannah's Dad, poised at a leapable distance from his daughter, smiled, as he watched carefully over Hannah conquest. He took much pleasure observing Hannah workout her faith by conquering one step and than another. Hannah was able to climb all the steps that led to the top of the slide, except the last one: it was more elevated than the others. Because Hannah's Daddy was watching her entire journey, he had already began moving toward her before she even cried out: "Daddy I can't reach it!" When she cried out, he instantly responded, **"Daddy will help you."**

How often have we cried out to our Heavenly
Father saying? "Daddy I can't reach it!"

I can't reach the peace spoken about in your Word; it seems this storm is too much

I can't reach your comfort I so desperately need after the loss of my loved one

I can't reach the hope needed to try again after another failure

I can't reach the forgiveness that is necessary to renovate my marriage

I can't reach the belief that my faith needs in order to experience healing

I can't reach my next… because there is a mountain of lack before me

I can't reach rest… because fighting is what I do best

In His Chambers

I can't reach good thoughts… because I keep rewinding the evil that happen to me
I can't reach the promise because I am exhausted from the journey

Daddy I need Your Help!
I Can't Reach It!

In the midst of so many I can'ts God says, "With man this is impossible, but with God all things are possible" **(Mark 10:27b)**.

Our Father, who knows all things, is
already positioned to help
already equipped with the best response to help
already able to perform the help
already full of power to help
already willing to help
and HE already knows I need help
before I even ask

GOD ALMIGHTY, who is our Daddy, when HE hears the prayers
of HIS children crying Abba, "I can't reach it!" HE says:

"Daddy will HELP you!"

In His Chambers

Mathew 6:8b-9a (ICB)

Your Father knows the things you need before you ask him. So when you pray, you should pray like this: "Our Father in heaven…"

The Lord is your Hero!!!
Jehovah Sabaoth
It is who HE is and
It is what HE does

Date:_____

_____
_____
_____
_____
_____
_____
_____
_____
_____
_____
_____
_____
_____
_____
_____
_____
_____
_____
_____
_____

In His Chambers

Psalm 12:1a (KJV)

For the Lord your God is he that goeth with you, to fight for you against your enemies, to save you.

Help, I need to be in YOUR presence...

my joy is being threaten

Date:_____

_____
_____
_____
_____
_____
_____
_____
_____
_____
_____
_____
_____
_____
_____

In His Chambers

Nehemiah 8:10c (KJV)

...for the joy of the Lord is your strength.

Psalm 16:11 (KJV)

Thou wilt shew me the path of life: in thy presence is fullness of joy; at thy right hand there are pleasures for evermore.

Help! I need a new song to sing...

about new seasons of victories, abundance and the promises of God

Date:_____

_____

_____

_____

_____

_____

_____

_____

_____

_____

_____

_____

_____

_____

_____

_____

_____

In His Chambers

Psalm 40:2-4a

He lifted me out of the pit of destruction, out of the sticky mud. He stood me on a rock. He made my feet steady. He put a new song in my mouth. It was a song of praise to our God. Many people will see this and worship him. Then they will trust the Lord. Happy is the person who trusts the Lord.

Help me stop believing who others say I am...
and start believing who the Great I AM says that I am

Date:_____

_____

_____

_____

_____

_____

_____

_____

_____

_____

_____

_____

_____

_____

_____

_____

In His Chambers

1 John 3:1 (ICB)

The Father has loved us so much! He loved us so much that we are called children of God.

Help, I need to stay spiritually awake...

so that I do not spend too much time wrestling with God's will

Date:_____

_____
_____
_____
_____
_____
_____
_____
_____
_____
_____
_____
_____
_____
_____
_____
_____
_____

In His Chambers

Genesis 28:6 (KJV)

And Jacob awaked out of his sleep, and he said, Surely the Lord is in this place; and I knew it not.

Help! God this is just evil and wrong...

How do I respond to such injustice?

Date:_____

_____

_____

_____

_____

_____

_____

_____

_____

_____

_____

_____

_____

_____

_____

_____

_____

_____

In His Chambers

Proverbs 8:32-33 (TLB)

And so, young men, listen to me, for how happy are all who follow my instructions. "Listen to my counsel—oh, do not refuse it—and be wise.

Help, I need to say something - I should be saying something...
Lord help me break the silence

Date:_____

_____

_____

_____

_____

_____

_____

_____

_____

_____

_____

_____

_____

_____

_____

_____

_____

_____

_____

In His Chambers

Romans 8:26 (KJV)

Likewise the Spirit also helpeth our infirmities: for we know not what we should pray for as we ought: but the Spirit itself maketh intercession for us with groanings which cannot be uttered.

But you, O Lord, are a shield around me; you are my glory, the one who holds my head high.

Psalm 119:71 (NLT)

Date:_____

_____
_____
_____
_____
_____
_____
_____
_____
_____
_____
_____
_____
_____
_____
_____
_____
_____
_____
_____
_____
_____
_____

In His Chambers

Help, I do not know how to resolve this conflict...
I need YOUR wisdom because my wisdom is definitely not working

Date:_____

_____
_____
_____
_____
_____
_____
_____
_____
_____
_____
_____
_____
_____
_____
_____

In His Chambers

I Chronicles 5:20 (ICB)

The men from the tribes of Manasseh, Reuben and Gad prayed to God in the war. They asked God to help them. So he helped them because they trusted him. He allowed them to defeat the Hagrites. And they also defeated all those who were with the Hagrites.

Then the man said to me, "Daniel, do not be afraid... I came to you because you have been praying. But the prince of Persia has been fighting against me for 21 days. Then Michael, one of the most important angels, came to help me..."

Daniel 10:12-13a (ICB)

Date:_____

_____

_____

_____

_____

_____

_____

_____

_____

_____

_____

_____

_____

_____

_____

_____

_____

_____

_____

_____

In His Chambers

Help! I need to trust in the powerful Word of God to resist temptation...

because when sin is finished
it brings death to relationships, trust,
confidence, dreams, respect, strength...

Date:_____

_____

_____

_____

_____

_____

_____

_____

_____

_____

_____

_____

_____

_____

_____

_____

_____

_____

In His Chambers

James 1:15 (KJV)

Then when lust hath conceived, it bringeth forth sin: and sin, when it is finished, bringeth forth death.

Thank God for those times when HIS help was accompanied by abundant grace, much mercy and unmerited favor...
(Be specific and free with the details of your praise)

Date:_____

_____
_____
_____
_____
_____
_____
_____
_____
_____
_____
_____
_____
_____
_____
_____
_____
_____
_____
_____
_____
_____
_____
_____

Help! My heart is broken into so many pieces...
I need the POTTER to make me again

Date:_____

_____
_____
_____
_____
_____
_____
_____
_____
_____
_____
_____
_____
_____
_____
_____
_____
_____

In His Chambers

Isaiah 63:1 (KJV)

The Spirit of the Lord God is upon me; because the Lord hath anointed me to preach good tidings unto the meek; he hath sent me to bind up the brokenhearted...

Help me to know that at the end of every successful distraction is theft, death and destruction...

but in following Jesus
there is life and
life more abundantly

Date:_____

_____
_____
_____
_____
_____
_____
_____
_____
_____
_____
_____
_____
_____

In His Chambers

John 10:8-11 (TLB)

All who came before me were thieves and robbers. But the true sheep did not listen to them. Yes, I am the gate. Those who come in through me will be saved. They will come and go freely and will find good pastures. The thief's purpose is to steal and kill and destroy. My purpose is to give them a rich and satisfying life. I am the good shepherd.

Help me to walk away with Godly certainty...
because I want the harvest that comes after this temptation

Date:_____

_____
_____
_____
_____
_____
_____
_____
_____
_____
_____
_____
_____
_____

In His Chambers

2 Chronicles 1:10-12 (TLB)

Now give me wisdom and knowledge to rule them properly, for who is able to govern by himself such a great nation as this one of yours. God replied, "Because your greatest desire is to help your people...I am giving you the wisdom and knowledge you asked for! And I am also giving you riches, wealth, and honor... And there will never again be so great a king in all the world!"

Lord, Thank YOU for helping me!

Write a praise letter to God for a time when sin was stealing your life and God's mercy, power and grace blocked it and made a way for you to escape!

Date:_____

_____

_____

_____

_____

_____

_____

_____

_____

_____

_____

_____

_____

_____

_____

_____

_____

_____

_____

_____

_____

_____

_____

In His Chambers

Help I need revival...
because I want improvement comeback, rejuvenation, recovery and resurrection

Date:_____

_____

_____

_____

_____

_____

_____

_____

_____

_____

_____

_____

_____

_____

_____

_____

_____

_____

_____

_____

In His Chambers

Psalm 138:7a (KJV)

Though I walk in the midst of trouble, thou wilt revive me...

Water Me Lord (page 1 of 2)

The length of this trail has dried my soil
My lamp burns dim and all that remains is a drought of oil
Iniquities have kidnapped my joy and my hope is all but a tease
This whole situation is breaking my heart and high jacking my peace
Water me Lord

Pour in YOUR Spirit
Pour on YOUR Oil
Pour out YOUR refreshing Word
Saturate my heart's crusty soil
So that I can bloom as YOU see me
Water me Lord
Water me

Pour out YOUR Word thick and not thin
Let it be a wellspring of living water from within
Marinade me in YOUR precious blood
Satisfy me with YOUR unconditional love
Quench my hunger with YOUR fire,
Feed my thirst with YOUR heart's desire

Pour in YOUR Spirit
Pour on YOUR Oil
Pour out YOUR refreshing Word
Saturate my heart's crusty soil
So that I can bloom as YOU see me
Water me Lord
Water me

Fruit has been scarce and the harvest few
Oh my Lord! Have mercy and rescue
Rooted near a river but there has been an extreme drought
How do I remain faithfully planted by a sea of doubt
Water me Lord

Water Me Lord

Pour in YOUR Spirit
Pour on YOUR Oil
Pour out YOUR refreshing Word
Saturate my heart's crusty soil
So that I can bloom as YOU see me
Water me Lord
Water me

YOU created me to be fruitful and to glorify YOUR name
And as long as I put my trust in YOU, I will never be ashamed
I will lean on your WORD because I know YOU do not lie
Father come soon because my inner man is peak summer dry
I will wait on YOU, although a cloud I can not trace
Because YOU can command rocks to gush water in a desert place
Water me Lord

Pour in YOUR Spirit
Pour on YOUR Oil
Pour out YOUR refreshing Word
Saturate my heart's crusty soil
So that I can bloom as YOU see me
Water me Lord
Water me

How refreshingly good! YOU have commanded the seasons to rearrange. The fields of my heart now bloom with the joy of the former and latter rain. I stand in amazement of the harvest, it's double for the trouble. I endured the years stolen by the locus, caterpillar and palmerworm. My restored heart is saturated with gratitude and humility. Because YOU have abundantly poured out fresh oil and water.

Prayer: *Lord when I am thirsty for love, peace, joy, faith, kindness, gentleness, meekness, self-control and endurance, fill me full with YOUR Holy Spirit*

The Lord will give strength unto his people; the Lord will bless his people with peace...
Psalm 29:11 (KJV)

Date:_____

_____

_____

_____

_____

_____

_____

_____

_____

_____

_____

_____

_____

_____

_____

_____

_____

_____

_____

_____

_____

In His Chambers

Help me stay calm and act wisely...
because I do not want to lose the progress we have made

Date:_____

_____

_____

_____

_____

_____

_____

_____

_____

_____

_____

_____

_____

_____

_____

_____

_____

_____

In His Chambers

Proverbs 1:23 (TLB)

Come here and listen to me! I'll pour out the spirit of wisdom upon you and make you wise.

Help I cannot see YOU...
But I know YOU are here and YOU see me
El Roi: the God who sees me

Date:_____

_____

_____

_____

_____

_____

_____

_____

_____

_____

_____

_____

_____

_____

_____

_____

_____

_____

_____

_____

In His Chambers

Genesis 16:13-14a (NIV)

She gave this name to the Lord who spoke to her: "You are the God who sees me," for she said, "I have now seen the One who sees me." That is why the well was called Beer Lahai Roi...

Knowing this, that the trying of your faith worketh patience. But let patience have her perfect work, that ye may be perfect and entire, wanting nothing....

James 1:3-4 (KJV)

Date:_____

_____

_____

_____

_____

_____

_____

_____

_____

_____

_____

_____

_____

_____

_____

_____

_____

_____

_____

_____

_____

_____

In His Chambers

Lord I need help to pray with only one mind and...
that is the mind of Christ which is to love God first and to love others

Date:_____

_____

_____

_____

_____

_____

_____

_____

_____

_____

_____

_____

_____

_____

_____

_____

In His Chambers

I Corinthians 2:16 (TLB)

How could he? For certainly he has never been one to know the Lord's thoughts, or to discuss them with him, or to move the hands of God by prayer. But, strange as it seems, we Christians actually do have within us a portion of the very thoughts and mind of Christ.

Help I am so tempted to do it my way...
it sounds good now but
I know it will not end good

Date:_____

_____

_____

_____

_____

_____

_____

_____

_____

_____

_____

_____

_____

_____

_____

_____

_____

_____

In His Chambers

Romans 6:22-23 (NLT)

But now you are free from the power of sin and have become slaves of God. Now you do those things that lead to holiness and result in eternal life. For the wages of sin is death, but the free gift of God is eternal life through Christ Jesus our Lord.

Help me do ministry...
because faith, minds, hearts
lives, hopes, dreams, destinies
and souls are at risk

Date:_____

_____

_____

_____

_____

_____

_____

_____

_____

_____

_____

_____

_____

_____

_____

_____

_____

_____

In His Chambers

Luke 22:31-32 (NLT)

"Simon, Simon, Satan has asked to have you, to sift you like wheat, but I have pleaded in prayer for you that your faith should not completely fail. So when you have repented and turned to me again, strengthen and build up the faith of your brothers."

Help me be joyous for the abundant mercy and grace YOU continually show me...
and freely give mercy and grace to others

Date:_____

_____
_____
_____
_____
_____
_____
_____
_____
_____
_____
_____
_____

In His Chambers

Romans 5:15-17 (NLT)

But there is a great difference between Adam's sin and God's gracious gift. For the sin of this one man, Adam, brought death to many. But even greater is God's wonderful grace and his gift of forgiveness to many through this other man, Jesus Christ. And the result of God's gracious gift is very different from the result of that one man's sin. For Adam's sin led to condemnation, but God's free gift leads to our being made right with God, even though we are guilty of many sins. For the sin of this one man, Adam, caused death to rule over many. But even greater is God's wonderful grace and his gift of righteousness, for all who receive it will live in triumph over sin and death through this one man, Jesus Christ.

Help me to know that I am on YOUR team...

Great Jehovah always win

Date:_____

_____

_____

_____

_____

_____

_____

_____

_____

_____

_____

_____

_____

_____

_____

In His Chambers

Psalm 46:1-5 (TLB)

God is our refuge and strength, a tested help in times of trouble. And so we need not fear even if the world blows up and the mountains crumble...Let the oceans roar and foam; let the mountains tremble! There is a river of joy flowing through the city of our God—the sacred home of the God...God himself is living in that city; therefore it stands unmoved despite the turmoil everywhere. He will not delay his help...

Help me to know that God is always right...

I am His beloved and
I am the righteousness of God

Date:_____

_____
_____
_____
_____
_____
_____
_____
_____
_____
_____
_____
_____
_____
_____
_____

In His Chambers

Deuteronomy 33:12 (TLB)

Concerning the tribe of Benjamin, Moses said: "He is beloved of God and lives in safety beside him. God surrounds him with his loving care, and preserves him from every harm."

Help me to live by faith and walk by YOUR Spirit...
so that my confidence will boldly rest in, on and with YOU

Date:_____

_____

_____

_____

_____

_____

_____

_____

_____

_____

_____

_____

_____

_____

_____

_____

_____

_____

In His Chambers

Ezekiel 36:27 (KJV)

And I will put my spirit within you, and cause you to walk in my statutes, and ye shall keep my judgments, and do them.

Help me be a servant leader...

and a humble follower of Christ Jesus

Date:_____

_____

_____

_____

_____

_____

_____

_____

_____

_____

_____

_____

_____

_____

_____

_____

In His Chambers

Luke 22:25-26 (ICB)

But Jesus said to them, "The kings of the world rule over their people. Men who have authority over others are called 'very important.' But you must not be like that. The greatest among you should be like the youngest, and the leader should be like the servant.

Help me not to be so selfish...

because it is just not good and certainly not Christ like

Date:_____

_____
_____
_____
_____
_____
_____
_____
_____
_____
_____
_____
_____
_____
_____
_____
_____

In His Chambers

1 Corinthians 13:2 (TLB)

If I had the gift of prophecy and knew all about what is going to happen in the future, knew everything about everything, but didn't love others, what good would it do? Even if I had the gift of faith so that I could speak to a mountain and make it move, I would still be worth nothing at all without love.

Help me to respond in love with kindness and meekness...
by faith, in peace
and with gentleness

Date:_____

_____

_____

_____

_____

_____

_____

_____

_____

_____

_____

_____

_____

_____

_____

_____

_____

_____

In His Chambers

Galatians 5:22-23a (TLB)

But when the Holy Spirit controls our lives he will produce this kind of fruit in us: love, joy, peace, patience, kindness, goodness, faithfulness, gentleness and self control

Help me be patient...
because the seed of it is love
and the fruit of it is immeasurable

Date:_____

_____

_____

_____

_____

_____

_____

_____

_____

_____

_____

_____

_____

_____

_____

_____

_____

In His Chambers

James 1:2-4 (TLB)

Dear brothers, is your life full of difficulties and temptations? Then be happy, for when the way is rough, your patience has a chance to grow. So let it grow, and do not try to squirm out of your problems. For when your patience is finally in full bloom, then you will be ready for anything, strong in character, full and complete.

Help me know when my help is in the mouth of the prophet...
and not in the mouth of my own mind

Date:_____

_____

_____

_____

_____

_____

_____

_____

_____

_____

_____

_____

In His Chambers

I Kings 17:12-14 (ICB)

The woman answered, "As surely as the Lord your God lives, I tell you the truth. I have no bread. I have only a handful of flour in a jar. And I have only a little olive oil in a jug. I came here to gather some wood. I will take it home and cook our last meal. My son and I will eat it and then die from hunger." Elijah said to her, "Do not worry. Go home and cook your food as you have said. But first make a small loaf of bread from the flour you have. Bring it to me. Then cook something for yourself and your son. The Lord, the God of Israel, says, 'That jar of flour will never become empty. The jug will always have oil in it. This will continue until the day the Lord sends rain to the land.'"

Help me stay close to YOU Jesus...

especially when it means sacrificing my desires for YOUR will

Date:_____

_____

_____

_____

_____

_____

_____

_____

_____

_____

_____

_____

_____

_____

_____

_____

_____

In His Chambers

James 4:7-8a (ICB)

So give yourselves to God. Stand against the devil, and the devil will run away from you. Come near to God, and God will come near to you...

Help me to choose to honor the Lord with obedience...

rather than walking in my own comfort or other's approval or my need to be in control

Date:_____

_____

_____

_____

_____

_____

_____

_____

_____

_____

_____

_____

_____

_____

_____

_____

_____

_____

In His Chambers

I Samuel 15:22 (ICB)

What pleases the Lord more: burnt offerings and sacrifices or obedience? It is better to obey God than to offer a sacrifice...

Lord, thank YOU for sending help!

Write a thank you letter to someone (a police officer, restaurant server, cashier, store clerk, food pantry volunteer, health care worker, mail carrier, nurse, doctor, dentist and pastor...) that you know God sent your way to help you. If you can, give the letter to that person: it will be very encouraging to them.

Date:_____

_____
_____
_____
_____
_____
_____
_____
_____
_____
_____
_____
_____
_____
_____
_____
_____
_____
_____
_____
_____
_____

O my soul, why be so gloomy and discouraged? Trust in God! I shall again praise him for his wondrous help; he will make me smile again, for he is my God!

Psalm 43:5 (TLB)

Date:_____

_____
_____
_____
_____
_____
_____
_____
_____
_____
_____
_____
_____
_____
_____
_____
_____
_____
_____
_____
_____
_____
_____

Help me to accept Help...
to lighten the load on my love and on my loved ones and to expand the impact of my faith

Date:_____

_____
_____
_____
_____
_____
_____
_____
_____
_____
_____
_____
_____
_____
_____
_____
_____
_____

In His Chambers

Luke 22:41-43 (NLT)

He walked away, about a stone's throw, and knelt down and prayed, "Father, if you are willing, please take this cup of suffering away from me. Yet I want your will to be done, not mine." Then an angel from heaven appeared and strengthened him.

Help me to know that it is all about YOU, about YOUR Glory and about YOUR Will...
I can, I do and I will trust YOU

Date:_____

_____

_____

_____

_____

_____

_____

_____

_____

_____

_____

_____

_____

In His Chambers

Revelation 4:11 (KJV)

Thou art worthy, O Lord, to receive glory and honour and power: for thou hast created all things, and for thy pleasure they are and were created.

Isaiah 12:2 (NLT)

See, God has come to save me. I will trust in him and not be afraid. The Lord God is my strength and my song; he has given me victory."

The Weapons of the Liar (Satan):
Disconnect *(page 1 of 2)*

The liar would have you believing that there is a time for plausible DISCONNECT
The liar will present evidence that forsaking the assembly will have little, to no effect

The liar will announce, it is better for you to be left alone during "this kind" of test
No one wants to smell the stench of your condition that is robbing you of your best

The truth is, with every temptation to believe that disconnect works, GOD has a way of escape
And no matter how long you have been away from the Father, your sonship is never up for debate

Isolated, we remove ourselves from the path of family, friends or the preacher coming our way
And should they all pass you by, GOD will send a
Good Samaritan to serve and save the day

The truth is, "many hands make light work" and two walking together is much better than one
When the one falls, the other can lift her up and together they can battle until victory is won

In His Chambers

The Weapons of the Liar (Satan):
Disconnect

If there are two, then they can encourage and protect each
other by combatting spine to spine
If there are three, then it is even harder to lose, as
long as the three remain entwine

The liar would have you believe that a "self-made" anything
is a possible reality
The truth is, all that you have is given and will be returned
on the day of your finality

The liar would have you believe that we can
experience love, joy and peace anywhere – at anytime
But the truth is, such fruit is only promised if we remain
connected to Jesus Christ, the True Vine

John 15:5 (ICB)

**I (Jesus) am the vine, and you are the branches. If a person remains
in me and I remain in him, then he produces much fruit. But without
me he can do nothing.**

Prayer: Lord Jesus, HELP me stay connected to you,
your word, your will and your people: especially
now since it seems so acceptable, comparable
and convenient to remain disconnected

Help me to hate evil and love good...

God is good!

Date:_____

_____

_____

_____

_____

_____

_____

_____

_____

_____

_____

_____

_____

_____

_____

_____

_____

In His Chambers

Amos 5:15 (TLB)

Hate evil and love the good...

Mathew 19:17 (KJV)

...Why callest thou me good? there is none good but one, that is, God...

Now do not worry about a thing, my child; I'll handle all the details, for everyone knows what a wonderful person you are.

Ruth 3:11 (TLB)

Date:_____

_____
_____
_____
_____
_____
_____
_____
_____
_____
_____
_____
_____
_____
_____
_____
_____
_____
_____
_____
_____

In His Chambers

Help me seek to serve the kingdom of God first and love God first...
and trust that everything else I need HE will provide

Date:_____

_____

_____

_____

_____

_____

_____

_____

_____

_____

_____

_____

_____

_____

_____

_____

_____

_____

_____

In His Chambers

Mathew 6:33 (ICB)

The thing you should want most is God's kingdom and doing what God wants. Then all these other things you need will be given to you.

Help sometimes comes in stopping to enjoy God's riches...

parents, children and friends
salvation, love and mercy
grace, peace and Jesus

Date:_____

_____

_____

_____

_____

_____

_____

_____

_____

_____

_____

_____

_____

_____

_____

_____

_____

In His Chambers

I Timothy 6:17 (NIV)

Command those who are rich in this present world not to be arrogant nor to put their hope in wealth, which is so uncertain, but to put their hope in God, who richly provides us with everything for our enjoyment.

Help me put away childish ways...

so I can eat the meat of PURPOSE and taste the sweet fruit of LOVE

Date:_____

_____

_____

_____

_____

_____

_____

_____

_____

_____

_____

_____

_____

_____

In His Chambers

I Corinthians 13:4-5, 11, 13 (NLT)

Love is patient and kind. Love is not jealous or boastful or proud or rude. It does not demand its own way. It is not irritable, and it keeps no record of being wronged. When I was a child, I spoke and thought and reasoned as a child. But when I grew up, I put away childish things. Three things will last forever—faith, hope, and love—and the greatest of these is love.

Help me stop resuscitating past hurts with my bitterness...

and start devouring the refreshing, healing elixir of forgiveness

Date:_____

_____

_____

_____

_____

_____

_____

_____

_____

_____

_____

_____

_____

_____

_____

_____

_____

_____

In His Chambers

Luke 11:4 (VOICE)

And forgive us for our wrongs, for we forgive those who wrong us. And lead us away from temptation. And save us from the evil one.

I have been in this place too long: please spray some RAID on my pride...
because I need Help!

Date:_____

_____

_____

_____

_____

_____

_____

_____

_____

_____

_____

_____

_____

_____

_____

_____

_____

In His Chambers

2 Chronicles 34:27 (NLT)

You were sorry and humbled yourself before God when you heard his words against this city and its people. You humbled yourself and tore your clothing in despair and wept before me in repentance. And I have indeed heard you, says the Lord.

Help me out of this cycle of sin because it is decomposing my life...
I know you have better for me

Date:_____

_____
_____
_____
_____
_____
_____
_____
_____
_____
_____
_____
_____
_____
_____
_____
_____
_____

In His Chambers

Hebrews 6:9 (KJV)

But, beloved, we are persuaded better things of you, and things that accompany salvation...

Help me stop enabling and start helping...
by following the Holy Spirit's lead

Date:_____

_____

_____

_____

_____

_____

_____

_____

_____

_____

_____

_____

_____

_____

_____

_____

_____

_____

_____

_____

In His Chambers

Zechariah 4:6c (KJV)

...Not by might, nor by power, but by my spirit...

Help me not be too disappointed for too long...
especially when rejection is Divine redirection

Date:_____

_____

_____

_____

_____

_____

_____

_____

_____

_____

_____

_____

_____

_____

_____

_____

_____

_____

In His Chambers

Jeremiah 29:11-13 (NLT)

"For I know the plans I have for you," says the Lord. "They are plans for good and not for disaster, to give you a future and a hope. In those days when you pray, I will listen. If you look for me wholeheartedly, you will find me."

I waited patiently for the Lord to help me, and he turned to me and heard my cry. He lifted me out of the pit of despair, out of the mud and the mire. He set my feet on solid ground and steadied me as I walked along.

Psalm 40:1-2 (NLT)

Date:_____

_____

_____

_____

_____

_____

_____

_____

_____

_____

_____

_____

_____

_____

_____

_____

_____

_____

_____

_____

In His Chambers

Help! I need confidence...
I am afraid of failing and falling again

Date:_____

_____

_____

_____

_____

_____

_____

_____

_____

_____

_____

_____

_____

_____

_____

_____

_____

_____

_____

In His Chambers

Hebrews 10:35-36 (ICB)

So do not lose the courage that you had in the past. It has a great reward. You must hold on, so you can do what God wants and receive what he has promised.

An "All Things New" Ending

I do not want a moment to stop experiencing YOU
I want the courage it takes to press forward and to break through
Break through to the next level of loving YOU
Break through to less of me and more of "What would Jesus do?"

I do not want to pick up pieces and restart again
I want to step over remains of walls and enter in
Enter in to great victories and the Father's promise land
Enter in to sweet fruit, milk harvest and God's divine plan

I do not want to write another beginning
I want the faith to leap into a new ending
A new ending of risk and daring to believe God's good report
A new ending of responsibility, strength, forgiveness and support

I do not want to say "next" like a cashier with no one in line
I want to say, "WOW, look what the Lord has done this time"
This time, we have broken bad habits of isolation and insecurity
This time we started new customs of faith walks and loving honesty

I do not want to run from processes, birthing pains and labor
I want to inhale courage and taste the "abundant life" flavors
Life's flavor of hope, creativity, commitment, help and treasury
Life's flavor of spice, servitude, beauty, sacrifice and intimacy

I do not want a new day with the same stagnant beginning
I want help, faith and power to experience an "all things new" ending

Therefore if any man be in Christ, he is a new creature: old things are
passed away; behold, all things are become new
2 Corinthians 5:17 (KJV)

In His Chambers

Help me to know that I have access to power...

that is not
of "this" world

Date: _____

_____

_____

_____

_____

_____

_____

_____

_____

_____

_____

_____

_____

_____

In His Chambers

2 Kings 6:15-17 (NLT)

When the servant of the man of God got up early the next morning and went outside, there were troops, horses, and chariots everywhere. "Oh, sir, what will we do now?" the young man cried to Elisha. "Do not be afraid!" Elisha told him. "For there are more on our side than on theirs!" Then Elisha prayed, "O Lord, open his eyes and let him see!" The Lord opened the young man's eyes, and when he looked up, he saw that the hillside around Elisha was filled with horses and chariots of fire.

Help me to rest from my labor...

and labor to do YOUR good works

Date:_____

In His Chambers

Matthew 11:28-29 (KJV)

Come unto me, all ye that labour and are heavy laden, and I will give you rest.
Take my yoke upon you, and learn of me; for I am meek and lowly in heart: and
ye shall find rest unto your souls.

For whatever God says to us is full of living power...
Hebrews 4:12 (TLB)

Date:_____

_____

_____

_____

_____

_____

_____

_____

_____

_____

_____

_____

_____

_____

_____

_____

_____

_____

_____

_____

_____

_____

_____

Blessed be God, who didn't turn away when I was praying and didn't refuse me his kindness and love...

Psalm 66:20 (TLB)

Date:_____

_____

_____

_____

_____

_____

_____

_____

_____

_____

_____

_____

_____

_____

_____

_____

_____

_____

_____

_____

_____

_____

_____

_____

Help me to walk by the truth I believe...
and not by the circumstances I see

Date:_____

_____

_____

_____

_____

_____

_____

_____

_____

_____

_____

_____

_____

_____

_____

_____

_____

In His Chambers

Mark 5:25-28 (TLB)

In the crowd was a woman who had been sick for twelve years with a hemorrhage. She had suffered much from many doctors through the years and had become poor from paying them, and was no better but, in fact, was worse. She had heard all about the wonderful miracles Jesus did, and that is why she came up behind him through the crowd and touched his clothes. For she thought to herself, "If I can just touch his clothing, I will be healed."

Help me to know I was created for "This"...

and YOU have equipped me with all I need to finish "This"

Date:_____

_____

_____

_____

_____

_____

_____

_____

_____

_____

_____

_____

_____

_____

_____

_____

_____

_____

In His Chambers

Philippians 1:6 (NLT)

And I am certain that God, who began the good work within you, will continue his work until it is finally finished on the day when Christ Jesus returns.

Help, I need to follow the Good Shepherd to the place where I shall not want for grace, for love, for peace, for new life, for restoration, for strength, for purpose, for truth, for power nor for rest...

Help me know that
The Lord is my Good Shepherd

Date:_____

_____
_____
_____
_____
_____
_____
_____
_____
_____
_____
_____
_____
_____
_____
_____
_____

In His Chambers

Psalm 23:1 (TLB)

Because the Lord is my Shepherd, I have everything I need!

For the Lamb standing in front of the throne will feed them and be their Shepherd and lead them to the springs of the Water of Life. And God will wipe their tears away."

Revelation 7:17 (TLB)

Date:_____

_____

_____

_____

_____

_____

_____

_____

_____

_____

_____

_____

_____

_____

_____

_____

_____

_____

_____

_____

_____

In His Chambers

Help! Lead me out of this cycle of under-use, misuse, overuse and abuse...

because a cycle of blessings is waiting for me at the off ramp

Date:_____

_____
_____
_____
_____
_____
_____
_____
_____
_____
_____
_____
_____
_____
_____
_____
_____
_____

In His Chambers

Deuteronomy 2:2-3 (KJV)

And the Lord spake unto me, saying, Ye have compassed this mountain long enough: turn you northward.

Let thine hand help me; for I have chosen thy precepts...
Psalm 119:173 (KJV)

Date:_____

_____
_____
_____
_____
_____
_____
_____
_____
_____
_____
_____
_____
_____
_____
_____
_____
_____
_____
_____
_____
_____
_____
_____
_____
_____

In His Chambers

Help me to pray and walk by faith...
and be a conduit for YOUR miracles

Date:_____

_____

_____

_____

_____

_____

_____

_____

_____

_____

_____

_____

_____

_____

In His Chambers

Mathew 9:27-30a (KJV)

And when he was come into the house, the blind men came to him: and Jesus saith unto them, Believe ye that I am able to do this? They said unto him, Yea, Lord. Then touched he their eyes, saying, According to your faith be it unto you. And their eyes were opened...

Jesus told them. "For if you had faith even as small as a tiny mustard seed, you could say to this mountain, 'Move!' and it would go far away. Nothing would be impossible..."

Matthew 17:20b (TLB)

Date:_____

_____

_____

_____

_____

_____

_____

_____

_____

_____

_____

_____

_____

_____

_____

_____

_____

_____

_____

_____

_____

The Weapons of the Liar
(Satan): Causality

The liar would have you believe that there is no
CAUSALITY between intangible thoughts and tangible experiences
That life is merely a sequence of random events and
inevitable coincidences

The TRUTH is, everything seen was first the vision in a mind: the
mind of God or HIS creation
And as a man thinks so is he and as the king thinks soon follows
the nation

The liar would have you believe that because you are having a
difficult time doing something, that it cannot be God's will
The TRUTH is, that God's will was in Jesus raising
Lazarus from the dead and in Jesus dying on Golgotha's hill

The TRUTH is, no matter if you are inhaling a victory or exhaling
the last breath of your story,
Putting your trust in the Lord will make all things work out for
your good and for HIS glory

The Weapons of the Liar
(Satan): Causality *(page 2 of 2)*

The liar would have you believe that the frequency and
intensity of temptation
has nothing to do with the proximity of your breakthrough,
destiny or next elevation

The TRUTH is, the closer you get to birthing each step ordered by
God; your life becomes like an unconsumed burning bush
The pain intensifies, the enemy's attacks become personal and you
will search for help when it is really a time to give birth and push

The TRUTH is, that your epidural for destiny's labor pains are not
in pharmacies created by the hands of man
Your remedies are love, prayer and total submission because these
weapons will always topple the enemy's plan

Prayer: Lord Jesus, help us to know that our worship and obedience
causes Godly experiences and we want our lives filled with B.A.M.
(**B**lessings **A**nd **M**iracles)

Jonah 3:10 (NLT)
*When God saw what they had done and how they had put a stop to their
evil ways, he changed his mind and did not carry out the destruction
he had threatened.*

Help me to live and say no to this addiction...
and yes to HELP

Date:_____

_____
_____
_____
_____
_____
_____
_____
_____
_____
_____
_____
_____
_____
_____
_____
_____
_____
_____
_____
_____
_____

In His Chambers

John 8:36 (KJV)

If the Son therefore shall make you free, ye shall be free indeed.

When I was helpless, he saved me. I said to myself, "Relax, because the Lord takes care of you."

Psalm 116:6b-7 (ICB)

Date:_____

_____

_____

_____

_____

_____

_____

_____

_____

_____

_____

_____

_____

_____

_____

_____

_____

_____

_____

_____

_____

_____

_____

In His Chambers

Help me just to trust YOU and do "it" now...
even if I am afraid, uncomfortable and anxious

Date:_____

_____

_____

_____

_____

_____

_____

_____

_____

_____

_____

_____

_____

_____

_____

In His Chambers

I Kings 17:12-14 (ICB)

The woman answered, "As surely as the Lord your God lives, I tell you the truth. I have no bread. I have only a handful of flour in a jar. And I have only a little olive oil in a jug. I came here to gather some wood. I will take it home and cook our last meal. My son and I will eat it and then die from hunger." Elijah said to her...But first make a small loaf of bread...Bring it to me. Then cook something for yourself and your son. The Lord, the God of Israel, says, 'That jar of flour will never become empty. The jug will always have oil in it...

Enough! With the laziness and blaming the devil for your choices
Be done with pointing your finger at the pressure of your peers'
voices
It is your voice that is stuck on repeat:
Grinding in behaviors, attitudes, thoughts and comfort zones of
defeat
It is your inside voice that is creating this realm of unproductive
realities
Evict your pride, divorce your wickedness and bring yourself to
your knees
Change the frequency, turn the page or download a new app
I am telling you now! Whether you like it or not, we are done with
that

You promised me! We had this conversation before
We both agreed that you would not do this anymore
Yet, here we are again, stuck at change's door
Stuck staring, Stuck questioning,
Stuck trembling in our faith,
Stuck, still trying to decide what to do
I am done! And I am not talking to you anymore
I have one hand cuffed to you, and one foot holding the door
Kicking and screaming we are both going through
You are screaming and I am dreaming
You have your eyes looking down at the drop
I have my eyes looking up at the mountaintop

Myself keeps telling me circumstances and conditions are not quite right
That sleeping in is better and that rest, not work, should be done at night
I do not expect progress without change,
Nor fruitfulness without an abundance rain
I have told you once and I am telling you twice
And now—I am done being patient and nice
I do not expect to conquer new territories without loss
I do not expect to evolve without God's Holy Spirit as my boss
Despite the fact that adversity masks the face of liberty
Crossing over now has become an absolute necessity
The next time I am in this mirror, me and myself will not be the same
Because Me, Myself and I are done playing these foolish mind games
Kicking & screaming the book will be done
Spiritual, mental and physical health becomes number one
Kicking & screaming victim mindsets are gone
I will forgive others and myself - so I can move on
I will not solely depend on self
But I will ask, seek and knock for help
I will prime over my past and paint something new
I will halt flesh-centered behavior and think more of YOU
I will speak life no matter how near the shadow of death
I will believe YOUR report despite how much time others say is left

KICKING & SCREAMING *(page 3 of 3)*

Kicking & screaming I will seek counseling for my marriage and grief

I will trust and pursue the Lord to convert my unbelief

I will say NO so that generational curses can be broken

I will say YES so that generational blessings are spoken

Kicking & screaming I will not leave my harvest on the field

I will trust, toil and obey until I see God's good plans fulfilled

Kicking and screaming I will keep my devotional and prayer time

I will be intentional about keeping Jesus and His works on my mind

Kicking & screaming I will stretch beyond stunting traditions and excuses - to experience something new

Kicking and screaming me, myself and I will love, serve and summit to YOU

Prayer: Lord help me to move forward and obey you even when everything inside me is KICKING & SCREAMING

In His Chambers

Luke 5:4-5 (NLT)

When he had finished speaking, he said to Simon, "Now go out where it is deeper, and let down your nets to catch some fish." "Master," Simon replied, "we worked hard all last night and didn't catch a thing. <u>But if you say so, I'll let the nets down again.</u>"

Help me set my mind on things above...

and think of the goodness I have and will experience

Date:_____

_____

_____

_____

_____

_____

_____

_____

_____

_____

_____

_____

_____

_____

_____

_____

In His Chambers

Philippians 4:8 (TLB)

And now, brothers, as I close this letter, let me say this one more thing: Fix your thoughts on what is true and good and right. Think about things that are pure and lovely, and dwell on the fine, good things in others. Think about all you can praise God for and be glad about.

Help, I do not know what to do next...

direct my steps to the next good thing YOU have planned for me

Date:_____

_____

_____

_____

_____

_____

_____

_____

_____

_____

_____

_____

_____

_____

_____

_____

_____

_____

_____

_____

_____

In His Chambers

Psalm 37:23 (KJV)

The steps of a good man are ordered by the Lord: and he delighteth in his way.

In His Chambers (page 1 of 3)

(Nearly every page of this journal has the tag phrase "In His Chambers". His Chambers refers to a small closet in my home that has been set apart as a place for prayer, studying, devotional and Bible reading. This place, is the place, where I am learning the love language and ways of the Trinity. The place where I leave my burdens and concerns for maintenance. It is where I can turn to my left and be encourage by a note card that I scribbled a scripture on.

This poem captures the heart of the closet that I affectionately call His Chamber.)

I will go into the chamber of my Lord
And hear His gracious calming voice
His voice is full of mercy
His voice is full of truth
His voice is full of authority
When my beloved speaks all things present and future, living or dead, in heaven or earth, hearing or deaf, seeing or blind, angelic or demonic, tangible or intangible awaits to accomplish His Word
His Word "fulfills the mission it was sent out to accomplish"
Therefore, I will rest my thoughts on the pillow of His Word
I will trust in the merciful, omniscient, omnipotent voice of my beloved Lord

In His Chamber, I hear
Taste and see that I am good
I love you with an everlasting love
You are the apple of my eye
I have lived and died and live for you
I will bless your comings and your goings
I pledge my presence to you forever and for always
I have prepared wisdom and understanding for your delight

In His Chambers

In His Chamber, I hear
My Lord singing songs of love and victory over me
I hear the assurance that no weapon formed against me will prosper
And that My grace is sufficient
I hear, this battle is not yours, I will personally bring you victory
I hear, my Beloved saying come and dine with the Master
Come learn to enjoy the Rock of Your Salvation
Come rest under the Son and lay in my plush meadows

In His Chambers, I come
I come humbly because You have given Yourself for me
I come boldly because You invited me
I come childlike because You adopted me
I come worshipping because You alone are worthy
I come praising because I have breath
I come into His Chamber because I need to be near You
That I may know You, Your ways, Your love language,
Your purpose and Your good plans

I come to feast with the Creator of Love
And with the Lord of Peace and the Lord who is my Hero
The Lord who is my garment of praise
And a living well of new beginnings
In His Chamber, I lock eyes with the kindness of my Lord
I see the Lord, my Good Shepherd
He leads me down paths of fruitfulness, sweetness,
Paths that are ripe with living, giving and loving

In His Chambers

Paths that illuminate steps of strengthen, wisdom, mercy and grace
Paths that refresh, heal, restore, redeem, replenish and reset harvest seasons

The chamber of my Lord has been open by the shed blood of Jesus
Jesus stands at the door of the chamber of our hearts
Knocking out the tune "Come into my heart, Come into my heart, Come into my heart Lord Jesus, Come into day, Come into stay, Come into my heart Lord Jesus..."
Come into His Chamber and present yourselves to the Lord
Just as you are - come and know Love qua Love

Jehovah is In His Chamber

Come now
Come often
Come in - close the door - stay a while

In His Chambers

Help! I want to walk in the purpose, power and will of God...

Look at Je (Jesus)
Look to HG (Holy Ghost)
Reach for G (God)
It is all in the Trinity

Date:_____

_____

_____

_____

_____

_____

_____

_____

_____

_____

_____

_____

_____

_____

In His Chambers

Acts 3:5-7 (ICB)

The man looked at them; he thought they were going to give him some money. But Peter said, "I do not have any silver or gold, but I do have something else I can give you: By the power of Jesus Christ from Nazareth— stand up and walk!" Then Peter took the man's right hand and lifted him up. Immediately the man's feet and ankles became strong.

Thou wilt shew me the path of life: in thy presence is the fullness of joy; at thy right hand there are pleasures for evermore...

Psalm 16:11 (KJV)

Date:_____

_____

_____

_____

_____

_____

_____

_____

_____

_____

_____

_____

_____

_____

_____

_____

_____

_____

_____

_____

In His Chambers

Lord, since I cannot go back, help me to move forward...

because standing still is harder than I thought

Date:_____

_____

_____

_____

_____

_____

_____

_____

_____

_____

_____

_____

_____

_____

_____

_____

_____

_____

In His Chambers

Psalm 46:10-11 (ICB)

God says, "Be still and know that I am God. I will be praised in all the nations. I will be praised throughout the earth." The Lord of heaven's armies is with us. The God of Jacob is our protection.

Help me Lord to stop being so negative about so many things...
especially when all things will work together for my good

Date:_____

_____

_____

_____

_____

_____

_____

_____

_____

_____

_____

_____

_____

_____

_____

_____

_____

_____

In His Chambers

Romans 8:28 (NLT)

And we know that God causes everything to work together for the good of those who love God and are called according to his purpose for them.

Help deliver me from evil...
The Lord, He is a Mighty Warrior and an Enemy to my enemy

Date:_____

_____

_____

_____

_____

_____

_____

_____

_____

_____

_____

_____

_____

_____

_____

_____

_____

_____

_____

In His Chambers

Psalm 28:6-8 (NLT)

Praise the Lord! For he has heard my cry for mercy. The Lord is my strength and shield. I trust him with all my heart. He helps me, and my heart is filled with joy. I burst out in songs of thanksgiving. The Lord gives his people strength...

What a wonderful God we have—he is the Father of our Lord Jesus Christ, the source of every mercy, and the one who so wonderfully comforts and strengthens us in our hardships and trials. And why does he do this? So that when others are troubled, needing our sympathy and encouragement, we can pass on to them this same help and comfort God has given us...

Hebrews 4:16 (NIV)

Date:_____

_____

_____

_____

_____

_____

_____

_____

_____

_____

_____

_____

_____

_____

_____

_____

_____

_____

_____

In His Chambers

Help! I am a single parent and I am tired...

I know I can not stop but I sure could use a recess

Date:_____

_____

_____

_____

_____

_____

_____

_____

_____

_____

_____

_____

_____

_____

_____

In His Chambers

Matthew 11:29-30 (MSG)

"Are you tired? Worn out? Burned out on religion? Come to me. Get away with me and you'll recover your life. I'll show you how to take a real rest. Walk with me and work with me—watch how I do it. Learn the unforced rhythms of grace. I won't lay anything heavy or ill-fitting on you. Keep company with me and you'll learn to live freely and lightly."

Single Parent: GOD KNOWS *(page 1 of 2)*

Children will never know how many nights (for them) you paced your
bedroom floor
Nor the numerous prayers you have prayed as they casually walk out
the front door
They will never know how much patience it takes to teach each child
how to write, add and read
The persistency it takes to teach a child how to walk, to run, to hope,
to survive and believe

Children will never know
But God Knows

Children will never know the dreams you delayed nor the nightmares
you endured
Because weeping was for your night but the morning offered them joy
and much more
They will never know that many of the relationships that you cherish
and manage
Were not just for your growth and welfare but also for your children's
advantage

Children will never know
But God Knows

Children will never know that even when they move out the home and
are good and "grown"
How much you still labor in love for them in practice, in prayers, with
tears and groans
They will never know how disrupted you are when they make choices
that lead them astray
And even though your reserves are low you are available to them in any
possible way

Children will never know
But God Knows

Children will never know what you had to be forgiven for and who/ what you had to forgive
To ensure that they would make it and have the life & lifestyle they now live
They will never know the new clothes you walked by and the candy bars you ate
So that they could be warm, wear nice clothes and have food on their plate

Children will never know

But God Knows

Children will never know the tears you held back while they were complaining and crying
So you could model hope, courage, strength and the power to just keep going, trusting and trying
They will never know the price of your passion that laid the foundation they now build on and live in
Nor will they know the battles, knockouts and victories you have fought so that they could win

Children will never know

But God Knows

Your child, will never fully know what being the only natural parent flowering them really cost
What they do know is that without your village, love, faith, sacrifices, prayers and guidance, they would be lost
They will never know how you were able to continue to take and give what you did not have and more
But God knows and HE is faithful to reward

Children will never know

But God Knows

For the mountains may depart and the hills disappear, but my kindness shall not leave you. My promise of peace for you will never be broken, says the Lord who has mercy upon you...

Isaiah 54:10 (TLB)

Date:_____

_____

_____

_____

_____

_____

_____

_____

_____

_____

_____

_____

_____

_____

_____

_____

_____

_____

_____

_____

In His Chambers

Help I need to hear YOUR voice...

when YOU speak I am certain that it will happen

Date:_____

_____

_____

_____

_____

_____

_____

_____

_____

_____

_____

_____

_____

_____

_____

_____

_____

_____

_____

_____

In His Chambers

Ezekiel 12:2a (NKJV)

For I am the Lord. I speak, and the word which I speak will come to pass...

"Sir," they said, "give us that bread everyday of our lives!" Jesus replied, "I am the Bread of Life. No one coming to me will ever be hungry again. Those believing in me will never thirst.

John 6:34-35 (TLB)

Date:_____

_____

_____

_____

_____

_____

_____

_____

_____

_____

_____

_____

_____

_____

_____

_____

_____

_____

_____

_____

In His Chambers

Help me stop complaining...
especially when I should be thanking YOU for bringing me out, over, through and into so many blessings

(Start this journal page with, my Good Heavenly Father: thank you for **bringing me out** of_____; thank you for the time I **over** came my weakness for_____; thanks for being the_____break**through** I needed to continue; thanks for leading me **into** such an amazing relationship with my_____.)

Date:_____

_____

_____

_____

_____

_____

_____

_____

_____

_____

_____

_____

_____

In His Chambers

Philippians 2:13-14 (TLB)

For God is at work within you, helping you want to obey him, and then helping you do what he wants. In everything you do, stay away from complaining and arguing.

Help! I am blinded by my own prejudice, bias, unforgiveness and anger...

and have forgotten how to be gracious with love, mercy and kindness

Date:_____

_____

_____

_____

_____

_____

_____

_____

_____

_____

_____

_____

_____

In His Chambers

Mark 10:46-52 (ICB)

The blind man cried out, "Jesus, Son of David, please help me!" Many people scolded the blind man and told him to be quiet. But he shouted more and more, "Son of David, please help me!"... Jesus stopped and said, ... "What do you want me to do for you?" The blind man answered, "Teacher, I want to see again." Jesus said, "Go. You are healed because you believed."

Holy Spirit, help me worship...
I need to be in the presence of the KING of kings

Date:_____

_____

_____

_____

_____

_____

_____

_____

_____

_____

_____

_____

_____

_____

_____

_____

_____

_____

_____

_____

_____

In His Chambers

Psalm 89:15 (NLT)

Happy are those who hear the joyful call to worship, for they will walk in the light of your presence, Lord.

Help me with a promotion...
so that I can add to YOUR kingdom and my world

Date:_____

_____

_____

_____

_____

_____

_____

_____

_____

_____

_____

_____

_____

_____

_____

_____

_____

_____

_____

In His Chambers

Psalm 75:4-7 (TLB)

I warned the proud to cease their arrogance! I told the wicked to lower their insolent gaze and to stop being stubborn and proud. For promotion and power come from nowhere on earth, but only from God. He promotes one and deposes another.

Help me stop gossiping...
I am losing friends that I should be helping and praying for

Date:_____

_____

_____

_____

_____

_____

_____

_____

_____

_____

_____

_____

_____

_____

_____

_____

_____

_____

_____

_____

_____

In His Chambers

Proverbs 16:27-28 (NLT)

Scoundrels create trouble; their words are a destructive blaze. A troublemaker plants seeds of strife; gossip separates the best of friends.

Help me crucify my pride and love others...

and not love my pride and crucify others

Date:_____

_____

_____

_____

_____

_____

_____

_____

_____

_____

_____

_____

_____

_____

_____

_____

_____

_____

_____

In His Chambers

Mathew 9:19-21 (ICB)

Pride leads to destruction. A proud attitude brings ruin.

Help me not to judge the choice of others...

but rather love, pray and help my sisters & brothers

Date:_____

_____

_____

_____

_____

_____

_____

_____

_____

_____

_____

_____

_____

_____

_____

_____

_____

In His Chambers

Luke 7:47 (ICB)

I tell you that her many sins are forgiven. This is clear because she showed great love. But the person who has only a little to be forgiven will feel only a little love.

Help me to fight and see the real enemy...

and use more formidable weapons: faith, sacrifice, trust, love, forgiveness, mercy kindness and believing God's Word

Date:_____

_____

_____

_____

_____

_____

_____

_____

_____

_____

_____

_____

_____

_____

_____

_____

_____

In His Chambers

2 Corinthians 10:4 (ICB)

We fight with weapons that are different from those the world uses. Our weapons have power from God. These weapons can destroy the enemy's strong places...

Help me not to judge others...
but rather be an effectual and fervent prayer warrior for others

Date:_____

_____

_____

_____

_____

_____

_____

_____

_____

_____

_____

_____

_____

_____

_____

_____

_____

_____

_____

_____

In His Chambers

James 5:16 (ICB)

Confess your sins to each other and pray for each other. Do this so that God can heal you. When a good man prays, great things happen.

Help me see opportunities to be loving, kind and helpful to others...
so that I can help spread the Gospel

Date:_____

_____
_____
_____
_____
_____
_____
_____
_____
_____
_____
_____
_____
_____
_____
_____
_____
_____
_____
_____
_____

In His Chambers

John 13:35 (KJV)

By this shall all men know that ye are my disciples, if ye have love one to another.

Help me to listen for the silent screams of others...

and anoint me to be helpful
even when my presence and silence
is the best help I can offer

Date:_____

_____

_____

_____

_____

_____

_____

_____

_____

_____

_____

_____

_____

_____

In His Chambers

Luke 8:49-56 (TLB)

While he was still speaking to her, a messenger arrived from the Jairus's home with the news that the little girl was dead. "She's gone," he told her father; "there's no use troubling the Teacher now." But when Jesus heard what had happened, he said to the father, "Do not be afraid! Just trust me, and she'll be all right."

Help me stop fighting my help...

especially when my help comes from those who love me

Date:_____

_____

_____

_____

_____

_____

_____

_____

_____

_____

_____

_____

_____

_____

_____

_____

_____

In His Chambers

Mark 6:4-5 (TLB)

Then Jesus told them, "A prophet is honored everywhere except in his hometown and among his relatives and by his own family." And because of their unbelief he couldn't do any mighty miracles among them except to place his hands on a few sick people and heal them.

It is God himself who has made us what we are and given us new lives from Christ Jesus; and long ages ago he planned that we should spend these lives in helping others.

Ephesians 2:10 (TLB)

Date:_____

We Are Here to Help One Another

I was driving to Wednesday Night Bible Study, on my normal route, when the Holy Spirit caused me to notice the weariness on the face of a woman walking with a suitcase in the opposite direction-on the opposite side of the road. I knew it was the Holy Spirit because the moment I saw her, the internal battle began: to stop or not to stop, that was the question. Within 30 seconds, my excuses and logic were pinned to the mat by the Holy Spirit and I made a U-turn. *(Oh how I wish that all my wrestling matches with the Holy Spirit ended so quickly).*

With my biggest smile and with a tone of cautious sincerity, I asked the traveler, if she needed a ride. She slowly exhaled a yes and with the same urgency that I have seen my mother kick off her high heel shoes, the traveler began loading her bags and luggage into my car. The traveler had been walking from the local train station. Daphne looked at me with confusion and said, "The GPS on my phone keeps saying go straight." She was from Massachusetts and had completed her business at the Pennsylvania Convention Center and now was on route to visit her friend. So that I could use the GPS on my smartphone, I asked for the address of her destination.

We Are Here to Help One Another *(page 2 of 2)*

It turned out, that the street Daphne was looking for, was three blocks behind her. She had walked right by it. Her phone was giving her directions as if she was driving rather than walking. This made a big difference because the street she was looking for was a one-way street and the next right turn, if driving, was two blocks away. With my help, Daphne was at her destination in less than two minutes and I was glad that the Lord had given me the opportunity to help someone.

When you know the Holy Spirit is leading you to help someone, trust that you have already been equipped with everything you will need to help them, especially God's protection and provision. Helping, then becomes a matter of are you willing to trust and obey the Holy Spirit. Or in Daphne's case, are you willing to except unexpected help. Our fears can sometimes stop us from receiving help or being helped. Ask the Holy Spirit to open your eyes to this infallible truth: **we are all here to help one another.**

In His Chambers

Romans 8:26-28 (NLT)

And the Holy Spirit helps us in our weakness. For example, we don't know what God wants us to pray for. But the Holy Spirit prays for us with groanings that cannot be expressed in words. And the Father who knows all hearts knows what the Spirit is saying, for the Spirit pleads for us believers in harmony with God's own will. And we know that God causes everything to work together for the good of those who love God and are called according to his purpose for them.

Help me to pursue and recover those whom I love...
LORD at YOUR word
I will fight and see victory!

Date:_____

_____
_____
_____
_____
_____
_____
_____
_____
_____
_____
_____
_____
_____
_____
_____
_____
_____

In His Chambers

I Samuel 30:8 (ICB)

Then David prayed to the Lord. He said, "Should I chase the people who took our families? Will I catch them?" The Lord answered, "Chase them. You will catch them. You will succeed in saving your families."

Help me not to stay when I should go and go when I should stay...
and give me a heart of love and wisdom that knows the difference

Date:_____

_____

_____

_____

_____

_____

_____

_____

_____

_____

_____

_____

_____

_____

_____

_____

_____

_____

_____

_____

_____

In His Chambers

Psalm 43:3 (VOICE)

O my God, shine Your light and truth to help me see clearly...

Help me to know my help when YOU send it...

so I do not reject my blessings just because of the packaging

Date:_____

_____

_____

_____

_____

_____

_____

_____

_____

_____

_____

_____

_____

_____

_____

_____

_____

_____

_____

In His Chambers

John 4:10 (TLB)

He replied, "If you only knew what a wonderful gift God has for you, and who I am, you would ask me for some living water...

Help me to trust that YOUR timing is perfect...
I will actively prepare and wait courageously

Date:_____

_____

_____

_____

_____

_____

_____

_____

_____

_____

_____

_____

_____

_____

_____

_____

_____

_____

_____

_____

_____

_____

In His Chambers

Ecclesiastes 3:1 (KJV)

To every thing there is a season, and a time to every purpose...

Lord, thank YOU for sending help!

Write a thank you letter to someone (a brother, sister, mother-in-law, step-child, coach, teacher, ex-spouse, stepparent, neighbor ...) that you know God sent your way to help you. If you can, give the letter to that person: it will be a big encouragement.

Date:_____

_____

_____

_____

_____

_____

_____

_____

_____

_____

_____

_____

_____

_____

_____

_____

_____

_____

_____

_____

In His Chambers

Help me stop talking...
and start listening

Date:_____

_____

_____

_____

_____

_____

_____

_____

_____

_____

_____

_____

_____

_____

_____

_____

_____

_____

_____

_____

In His Chambers

James 1:19 (NLT)

Understand this, my dear brothers and sisters: You must all be quick to listen, slow to speak, and slow to get angry.

Help me not to be so callous toward those I love...
and those that love me

Date:_____

_____
_____
_____
_____
_____
_____
_____
_____
_____
_____
_____
_____
_____
_____
_____
_____

In His Chambers

Ezekiel 36:26 (ICB)

Also, I will teach you to respect me completely. I will put a new way to think inside you. I will take out the stubborn heart like stone from your bodies. And I will give you an obedient heart of flesh.

Help me not to worry about my children...

and trust that as
YOU were with me
YOU will be with them

Date:_____

In His Chambers

Isaiah 61:9 (KJV)

And their seed shall be known among the Gentiles, and their offspring among the people: all that see them shall acknowledge them, that they are the seed which the Lord hath blessed.

Pray for someone other than your family or your needs...
Your prayers may be the very HELP someone needs

Date:_____

_____

_____

_____

_____

_____

_____

_____

_____

_____

_____

_____

_____

_____

_____

_____

In His Chambers

James 5:16 (TLB)

Admit your faults to one another and pray for each other so that you may be healed. The earnest prayer of a righteous man has great power and wonderful results.

Help me be a Godly father...
and instruct my children in the ways and Word of the Lord

Date:_____

_____

_____

_____

_____

_____

_____

_____

_____

_____

_____

_____

_____

_____

_____

_____

In His Chambers

Deuteronomy 11:18-21a (ICB)

Place these words on your hearts. Get them deep inside you. Tie them on your hands and foreheads as a reminder. Teach them to your children. Talk about them wherever you are, sitting at home or walking in the street; talk about them from the time you get up in the morning until you fall into bed at night. Inscribe them on the doorposts and gates of your cities so that you'll live a long time, and your children with you...

Help me be a Godly mother...
and nurture my children to respect and honor God the Father, God the Son and God the Holy Spirit

Date:_____

_____

_____

_____

_____

_____

_____

_____

_____

_____

_____

_____

_____

_____

_____

_____

_____

In His Chambers

Proverbs 22:6 (AMP)

Train up a child in the way he should go [teaching him to seek God's wisdom and will for his abilities and talents], Even when he is old he will not depart from it.

Help! My marriage is imploding... and I am afraid of what could happen next

Date:_____

_____

_____

_____

_____

_____

_____

_____

_____

_____

_____

_____

_____

_____

_____

_____

_____

_____

_____

_____

_____

In His Chambers

Isaiah 41:12-13 (ICB)

You will look for your enemies. But you will not find them. Those who fought against you will vanish completely. I am the Lord your God. I am holding your right hand. And I tell you, 'Do not be afraid. I will help you.

At the end of seven years I, Nebuchadnezzar, looked up to heaven, and my sanity returned, and I praised and worshiped the Most High God and honored him who lives forever...

Daniel 4:34 (TLB)

Date:_____

_____

_____

_____

_____

_____

_____

_____

_____

_____

_____

_____

_____

_____

_____

_____

_____

_____

_____

In His Chambers

Help me to know that who I am connected to matters...
because it will influence what I will experience next

Date:_____

_____

_____

_____

_____

_____

_____

_____

_____

_____

_____

_____

_____

_____

_____

In His Chambers

2 Kings 2:9-10 (TLB)

Then they arrived on the other side Elijah said to Elisha, "What wish shall I grant you before I am taken away?" And Elisha replied, "Please grant me twice as much prophetic power as you have had." "You have asked a hard thing," Elijah replied. "If you see me when I am taken from you, then you will get your request. But if not, then you won't."

The Weapons of the Liar
(Satan): Rejection (page 1 of 3)

The liar would have you believe:

That REJECTION is not an event but rather a disease that is alive

That rejection is a condition or state of being and its effects can never die

The liar would have you believe:

That the rejecters know exactly what they are doing when they mock, doubt and deny you

But Jesus said to HIS rejecters, "FATHER forgive them for they know not what they do" (Luke 23:34)

The TRUTH is, rejection is less personal and more about divine chrysalis, purpose and transformation

It is an opportunity to develop a character of strength, persistency, consistency and dedication

It is a fitness moment to work out your faith in seasons of resistance, development and frustration

The liar would have you believe:

That the only fruit that is produced by rejection is loss, hopelessness, bitterness and malice

The TRUTH is, God can use rejection as momentum to move us from comforts, to pit, to prison and ultimately to the palace

(Genesis chapters 37-41)

In His Chambers

The Weapons of the Liar
(Satan): Rejection (page 2 of 3)

The TRUTH is, a good response to rejection is to rehearse God's Word in your mind over and over again
And press forward until you draw out victory, healing and wholeness from Jesus's hem *(Mark 5:25-34)*

The liar would have you believe:
That rejection caused by our choice to sin, will leave us judged, condemned and deservingly left alone
The TRUTH is, Jesus never leaves and HE will cause our accusers to walk away and drop their stones
The TRUTH is, Jesus will not sprinkle on sinful rejection condiments of shame, condemnation and regret
But HE will offer forgiveness, restoration, and a dance with GRACE you will never forget

The liar would have you believe:
That rejection is final and that resistance is futile – so tap out and just submit your acceptancy
The TRUTH is, even an unjust "NO" is overruled by mercy's continual outcries and acts of persistency
(Luke 18-1-8 & Mathew 20:29-34)

In His Chambers

The Weapons of the Liar
(Satan): Rejection (page 3 of 3)

The liar would have you believe:
That rejection is a one sided coin of loss, death or a strangler to one's self-worth
The TRUTH is, the labor pains of rejection are the only way our life's body can experience new birth

Rejection though disappointing and painful as it can be
Is truly a part of the price paid for a one way ticket to Divine Destiny

Prayer: LORD, help me to see rejection
from YOUR perspective

In His Chambers

Then Jesus asked them, "Didn't you ever read in the Scriptures: 'The stone rejected by the builders has been made the honored cornerstone; how remarkable! what an amazing thing the Lord has done... (Mathew 21:42 TLB)

Lord help my son...

know the height, depth, width and length of YOUR powerful love

Date:_____

_____

_____

_____

_____

_____

_____

_____

_____

_____

_____

_____

_____

_____

_____

_____

In His Chambers

Mark 9:15-25 (NLT)

...Teacher, I brought my son so you could heal him. He is possessed by an evil spirit that won't let him talk. And whenever this spirit seizes him, it throws him violently to the ground... Jesus said to them...Bring the boy to me...Have mercy on us and help us, if you can.".…"What do you mean, 'If I can'?" Jesus asked. "Anything is possible if a person believes." The father instantly cried out, "I do believe, but help me overcome my unbelief!"... Jesus...said. "I command you to come out of this child and never enter him again!"

And all thy children shall be taught of the Lord; and great shall be the peace of thy children...

Isaiah 54:13 (KJV)

Date:_____

_____

_____

_____

_____

_____

_____

_____

_____

_____

_____

_____

_____

_____

_____

_____

_____

_____

_____

_____

_____

Family of Aaron, trust the Lord. He is your helper and your protection.

Psalm 115:10 (TLB)

(Say this scripture aloud, but replace Aaron's name with your own)

Date:_____

_____
_____
_____
_____
_____
_____
_____
_____
_____
_____
_____
_____
_____
_____
_____
_____
_____
_____
_____
_____
_____

Lord help me give to the poor...

and give to those who have less and are treated as less

Date:_____

_____

_____

_____

_____

_____

_____

_____

_____

_____

_____

_____

_____

_____

In His Chambers

Mathew 25:37-40 (NLT)

"Then these righteous ones will reply, 'Lord, when did we ever see you hungry and feed you? Or thirsty and give you something to drink? Or a stranger and show you hospitality? Or naked and give you clothing? When did we ever see you sick or in prison and visit you?' "And the King will say, 'I tell you the truth, when you did it to one of the least of these my brothers and sisters, you were doing it to me!'

Help me to express thanksgiving to others...

because giving and kindness are the choices of love

Date:_____

_____

_____

_____

_____

_____

_____

_____

_____

_____

_____

_____

_____

_____

_____

_____

_____

In His Chambers

John 3:16 (KJV)

For God so loved the world, that he gave his only begotten Son, that whosoever believeth in him should not perish, but have everlasting life.

Help me be ready, willing and able to forgive others...
just as Christ has forgiven me

Date:_____

_____

_____

_____

_____

_____

_____

_____

_____

_____

_____

_____

_____

_____

_____

_____

_____

In His Chambers

Ephesians 4:32 (KJV)

And be ye kind one to another, tenderhearted, forgiving one another, even as God for Christ's sake hath forgiven you.

READ ME MY RIGHTS: Freedom

I have a right to Freedom
After all, Jesus died for me
I have a right to be free from bondage
So I will
Walk in freedom from addiction
Leap into freedom from unbelief and fear
Run freedom's race from cycles of insecurity, emotional abuse,
poverty, depression and oppression
So I will
Stand under the waterfall of the Anointed One
HIS oil will destroy the yokes
HIS voice will break the bands
HIS name will pardon
I have a right to Freedom
After all, Jesus was scorned and scourged for my liberty
So I will
Take communion as often as I can
And always remember that Jesus is the LAMB of freedom
The KING of kings whose decree is unchangeable
The JUDGE of judges whose ruling is immutable
The MASTER of masters whose emancipation is eternal
The LORD of lords whose authority is forever
Whom the SON has set free is free indeed
Oh Yes! You have a right to freedom
After all, Jesus died for you!

In His Chambers

It is clear that God has called you to a free life. Just make sure that you don't use this freedom as an excuse to do whatever you want to do and destroy your freedom. Rather, use your freedom to serve one another in love; that's how freedom grows. For everything we know about

God's Word is summed up in a single sentence: Love others as you love yourself. That's an act of true freedom. If you bite and ravage each other, watch out—in no time at all you will be annihilating each other, and where will your precious freedom be then? (Galatians 5:13-14 MSG)

Help me use the power of my inner and outer tongue...
to build and not to tear down

Date:_____

_____

_____

_____

_____

_____

_____

_____

_____

_____

_____

_____

_____

_____

_____

_____

_____

_____

_____

_____

_____

_____

In His Chambers

Proverbs 15:4 (NLT)

Gentle words are a tree of life; a deceitful tongue crushes the spirit.

Help me be kind to others...
because YOU are abundantly kind to me

Date:_____

_____
_____
_____
_____
_____
_____
_____
_____
_____
_____
_____
_____
_____
_____
_____

In His Chambers

Proverbs 3:3 (NLT)

Never let loyalty and kindness leave you! Tie them around your neck as a reminder. Write them deep within your heart.

231

He will bless them that fear the Lord, both small and great. The Lord shall increase you more and more, you and your children. Ye are blessed of the Lord which made heaven and earth.

Psalm 115:13-15 (KJV)

Date:_____

_____

_____

_____

_____

_____

_____

_____

_____

_____

_____

_____

_____

_____

_____

_____

_____

_____

_____

_____

The Weapons of the Liar
(Satan): Doubt

The liar would have you DOUBTING
God's goodness is more about the fruit of your labor and less about God's amazing grace
The liar would have you redacting scriptures declaring that with the blood of Jesus all sin is erased
The TRUTH is, it is God's love that suffocates the voice of condemnation
And burns off the dross of hopelessness, un-forgiveness, bitterness and stagnation

The liar would have you debating the question: where is the finish line for God's grace?
Is it at that shameful moment when your are standing in the spotlight of disgrace?
The liar would have you skimming this TRUTH: that God's grace is like the ocean floor
His grace submerges deeper… and deeper… and deeper the further you drift from shore
The lair would have you believing that the more grace you use the less there is to go around
The TRUTH of the matter is, that where sin is much, grace much more abounds

The lair would have you boasting, that grace is a reward for tipping the good versus evil scale
And that the measure of your good deeds is what keeps you from residing in hell

The Weapons of the Liar
(Satan): Doubt *(page 2 of 2)*

The TRUTH is, Grace, he is a beautiful soul mate to be received
with gratitude
Not earned by good works, laboring hours, sacrifices or a positive
attitude
The TRUTH is, Grace can only be powerful, purposeful and
administered by the superior
And that He, Grace, has two faces one that forgives and another
that empowers the inferior

The liar would have you believe that Grace, He is only for those
who help themselves or can give more
The TRUTH is, Grace, He will bring salvation, peace and love to
all whose heart is poor
The liar would have you believe, that Grace is only for those who
miss the mark upon their landing
The TRUTH is, Grace is not only for the fallen but He is also the
power that keeps us all standing

Prayer: Jesus, help me not to doubt the power
and truth of YOUR Amazing Grace

In His Chambers

Acts 20:32 (ICB)

**Now I am putting you in the care of God and the message about his grace. That
message is able to give you strength, and it will give you the blessings that God
has for all his holy people.**

Help! I want to be at the end of insisting that it always has to be my way...
God's way is the best way!

Date:_____

_____
_____
_____
_____
_____
_____
_____
_____
_____
_____
_____
_____
_____
_____
_____
_____

In His Chambers

1 Samuel 12:23-24 (ICB)

I will surely not stop praying for you. If I did, I would be sinning against the Lord. I will teach you what is good and right. But you must honor the Lord. You must always serve him with all your heart. Remember the wonderful things he did for you!

Help I want to give birth...

to a child
to a vision
to a good habit
to _____

Date:_____

_____
_____
_____
_____
_____
_____
_____
_____
_____
_____
_____
_____
_____
_____
_____
_____
_____
_____

In His Chambers

Psalm 37:5 (NLT)

Commit everything you do to the Lord. Trust him, and he will help you.

Help...

this book
this degree
this assignment
this season
this purpose
this plan
needs to be finished

Date:_____

_____

_____

_____

_____

_____

_____

_____

_____

_____

_____

_____

_____

_____

In His Chambers

Philippians 1:6 (MSG)

There has never been the slightest doubt in my mind that the God who started this great work in you would keep at it and bring it to a flourishing finish on the very day Christ Jesus appears.

For this cause we also, since the day we heard it, do not cease to pray for you, and to desire that ye might be filled with the knowledge of his will in all wisdom and spiritual understanding...

Colossians 1:9 (KJV)

Date:_____

_____

_____

_____

_____

_____

_____

_____

_____

_____

_____

_____

_____

_____

_____

_____

_____

_____

_____

In His Chambers

Help me to trust YOU and finish the process...

and not allow the process to finish me

Date:_____

_____
_____
_____
_____
_____
_____
_____
_____
_____
_____
_____
_____
_____
_____

In His Chambers

2 Corinthians 4:16-17 (ICB)

So we do not give up. Our physical body is becoming older and weaker, but our spirit inside us is made new every day. We have small troubles for a while now, but they are helping us gain an eternal glory. That glory is much greater than the troubles.

Help me Lord! I am too close to being finished and if I quit, there is too much at risk...
Lord share YOUR courage and strength with me

Date:_____

_____

_____

_____

_____

_____

_____

_____

_____

_____

_____

_____

_____

_____

_____

_____

_____

_____

In His Chambers

Philippians 1:6 (ICB)

God began doing a good work in you. And he will continue it until it is finished when Jesus Christ comes again. I am sure of that.

Help me do "it" again and again by faith...

until the will of the Lord is what my eyes see or until my ears hear "well done"

Date:_____ __

_____

_____

_____

_____

_____

_____

_____

_____

_____

_____

_____

_____

_____

In His Chambers

2 Kings 5:10,14 (ICB)

Elisha sent a messenger to Naaman. The messenger said, "Go and wash in the Jordan River seven times. Then your skin will be healed, and you will be clean."... So Naaman went down and dipped in the Jordan seven times. He did just as Elisha had said. Then Naaman's skin became new again. It was like the skin of a little boy. And Naaman was clean!

Help! Mary said to Jesus, my brother is dead...
No Mary, Lazarus has been repositioned to experience resurrection power

Date:_____

_____

_____

_____

_____

_____

_____

_____

_____

_____

_____

_____

_____

_____

_____

_____

_____

_____

_____

_____

In His Chambers

Philippians 3:10a (KJV)

That I may know him, and the power of his resurrection...

I dance, sing and shout (probably not as often as I should) about the battle Jesus fought and won for my salvation. I must honestly confess, I cannot fully measure nor comprehend the cost that Jesus paid for us to experience the rewards of HIS great victory.

The battle that proceeds victory often leaves us with post victory exhaustion, moments of isolation and/or only one minute to catch our breath before the next round of the fight begins; the enemy knows that birthing victory leaves us weak and vulnerable to the next voice we hear. What the ears of your mind hears, after victory, will influence your next experience. Especially, if you feel like you are battling alone. So, before you listen to anything you say to yourself about how tired you are or what you need to do to self-medicate/celebrate or reconnect, hear the Lord's answer to your cry for help, replenishment, support, validation and strength: **GET UP AND EAT.**

The children cry HELP! The Father instructs **GET UP AND EAT.** Be careful not to dismiss the Master's call to come and dine - especially when you are fragmented, fighting, fatigued, famished or finished. El Shaddai *(Genesis 49:25)* is saying come: to Sunday morning worship, to bible study, to retreat, to prayer or to small group - "come sit at the table with me and eat". If you are hungry for change or transformation - thirsty for rest and recovery - starving for peace, health or breakthrough come into GOD's presence. Come eat and be near the voice of God— there is power in HIS voice. His voice is HIS promise and all heavens and earth are under HIS commands. HIS voice reveals what HE has in mind for you: Come eat! Say the prayer called "GRACE" and dig in! HE is prepared for you and HE has been expecting you. Dig into HIS presence. GOD has prepared a table of blessing: Fatigue and Fear maybe in proximity but they will not eat at the table; these twins will starve to death in God's presence. The Good Shepherd's offspring will rest in green meadows, drink from quiet streams. The Lord says let ME be personally yours: your Hero, your Righteousness, your Savior, your Counselor, your Sound Mind, your Strength, your Living Water, your Bread of Life, your Provider, your Prince of Life, your Comforter, your Reconciliation and your Rest. In ME is everything you could ever need to **Live**, to **Move** and to have your **Being**.

Live in Peace † **Live** in Purpose † **Live** Abundance
Move onto to Victory † **Move** out of Grief † **Move** into Overcoming
Being Fruitful † **Being** Loving † **Being** Faithful † **Being** Forgiving
† **Being** Holy

Let **Faith** be your fork, **Love** be your spoon and **Hope** be your knife. Let the Father's will be your choice meat. The Holy Spirit is your waiter; you can ask for what you want but may I suggest that you ask the WAITER what HE recommends. HE knows what is in the Father's Store House and what is on the Father's heart for you. Take your time in the Father's presence: experience a 10-course meal with HIM and you! Sit not as a quest but as a KING's heir and feast on the goodness of God's presence. Converse with HIM while you eat—HE is your Father. In the presence of your FATHER is HIS HELP and in HIS HELP is the fruit of love, joy, peace, meekness, faith, kindness, gentleness, endurance and self-control. If there be any hope of these precious fruits flowing abundantly in your life than it is in coming to Daddy's table and dining. Not only before the battle but also after the victory.

GET UP AND EAT

When victory's postpartum symptoms of exhaustion, isolation and fatigue appear, do not sit outside the door of provision and celebration, but hear the still small voice of your Heavenly Father saying **GET UP and EAT**.

I Kings 19:1-8 (ICB)

*King Ahab told Jezebel everything Elijah had done. Ahab told her how Elijah had killed all the prophets with a sword. So Jezebel sent a messenger to Elijah. Jezebel said, "By this time tomorrow I will kill you. I will kill you as you killed those prophets. If I do not succeed, may the gods punish me terribly." When Elijah heard this, he was afraid. So he ran away to save his life...Elijah left his servant...Then Elijah walked for a whole day into the desert. He sat down under a bush and asked to die. Elijah prayed, "I have had enough, Lord. Let me die...Then Elijah lay down under the tree and slept. Suddenly an angel came to him and touched him. The angel said, "**Get up and eat**." Elijah saw near his head a loaf baked over coals and a jar of water. So he ate and drank. Then he went back to sleep. Later the Lord's angel came to him a second time. The angel touched him and said, "**Get up and eat**. If you do not, the journey will be too hard for you..."*

In His Chambers

Praise God for His Help...

Finish this statement: If it had not been for the Lord's help,_____. For example, if it had not been for the Lord's help, I would have not be able to parent such amazing children. Journal your gratitude below.

Date:_____

_____

_____

_____

_____

_____

_____

_____

_____

_____

_____

_____

_____

_____

_____

_____

_____

_____

_____

In His Chambers

Luke 18:27 (AMP)

But He said, "The things that are impossible with people are possible with God."

Praise God for His Help...

Finish this statement: Lord you sent_____to help me make it through a tough time in my life. This can be a person, an organization, a ministry or even a book. Journal your gratitude below.

Date:_____

_____

_____

_____

_____

_____

_____

_____

_____

_____

_____

_____

_____

_____

_____

_____

_____

In His Chambers

Psalm 34:5-6 (ICB)

Those who go to him for help are happy. They are never disgraced. This poor man called, and the Lord heard him. The Lord saved him from all his troubles.

Praise God for His Help...

Finish this statement: Lord you sent＿＿＿＿＿＿to help me live a better life. For example: Lord you sent my wife, husband, accountant, mentor, advisor, pastor, friend, mother-in-law... to help me live a better life. Journal your gratitude. If you can, please share this letter with that person or a relative of that person.

Date:＿＿＿＿＿＿＿

＿＿＿＿＿＿＿＿＿＿＿＿＿＿＿＿＿＿＿＿＿＿＿＿＿＿＿＿＿＿＿

＿＿＿＿＿＿＿＿＿＿＿＿＿＿＿＿＿＿＿＿＿＿＿＿＿＿＿＿＿＿＿

＿＿＿＿＿＿＿＿＿＿＿＿＿＿＿＿＿＿＿＿＿＿＿＿＿＿＿＿＿＿＿

＿＿＿＿＿＿＿＿＿＿＿＿＿＿＿＿＿＿＿＿＿＿＿＿＿＿＿＿＿＿＿

＿＿＿＿＿＿＿＿＿＿＿＿＿＿＿＿＿＿＿＿＿＿＿＿＿＿＿＿＿＿＿

＿＿＿＿＿＿＿＿＿＿＿＿＿＿＿＿＿＿＿＿＿＿＿＿＿＿＿＿＿＿＿

＿＿＿＿＿＿＿＿＿＿＿＿＿＿＿＿＿＿＿＿＿＿＿＿＿＿＿＿＿＿＿

＿＿＿＿＿＿＿＿＿＿＿＿＿＿＿＿＿＿＿＿＿＿＿＿＿＿＿＿＿＿＿

＿＿＿＿＿＿＿＿＿＿＿＿＿＿＿＿＿＿＿＿＿＿＿＿＿＿＿＿＿＿＿

＿＿＿＿＿＿＿＿＿＿＿＿＿＿＿＿＿＿＿＿＿＿＿＿＿＿＿＿＿＿＿

＿＿＿＿＿＿＿＿＿＿＿＿＿＿＿＿＿＿＿＿＿＿＿＿＿＿＿＿＿＿＿

＿＿＿＿＿＿＿＿＿＿＿＿＿＿＿＿＿＿＿＿＿＿＿＿＿＿＿＿＿＿＿

＿＿＿＿＿＿＿＿＿＿＿＿＿＿＿＿＿＿＿＿＿＿＿＿＿＿＿＿＿＿＿

In His Chambers

John 14:16-18 (ICB)

I will ask the Father, and he will give you another Helper. He will give you this Helper to be with you forever. The Helper is the Spirit of truth. The world cannot accept him because it does not see him or know him. But you know him. He lives with you and he will be in you.

Help, I want to know that I am right with God and that I will live eternity with HIM Jesus: I AM the Way, Truth and Life

For they do not understand that Christ has died to make them right with God. Instead, they are trying to make themselves good enough to gain God's favor by keeping...laws and customs, but that is not God's way of salvation. They do not understand that Christ gives to those who trust in him everything they are trying to get by keeping his laws. He ends all of that. For Moses wrote that if a person could be perfectly good and hold out against temptation all his life and never sin once, only then could he be pardoned and saved. But the salvation that comes through faith says, You do not need to search the heavens to find Christ...and You do not need to go among the dead to bring Christ back to life again. For salvation that comes from trusting Christ is already within easy reach of each of us; in fact, it is as near as our own hearts and mouths. **For if you tell others with your own mouth that Jesus Christ is your Lord and believe in your own heart that God has raised him from the dead, you will be saved. For it is by believing in his heart that a man becomes right with God; and with his mouth he tells others of his faith, confirming his salvation.**

...Anyone who calls upon the name of the Lord Jesus will be saved.

If this is your first time confessing your belief about Jesus birth, life, death and resurrection than this date:_____is your Spiritual Birthday

In His Chambers

About the Author

Arleen Geathers is the founder and owner of Inspirational Journals 4 U LLC. On her website: www.journalpower4u.com, you will find over 40 sustenance journals with various subject themes: prayer, gratitude, faith and trust. Her youth journal, a collaboration with her 12-year-old son, is an excellent way to introduce preteens and older to truths that will build their character. Her brand of journals are so much more than just lines on a page. With these journals, you will experience and unforgettable conversation as you share your written voice (journaling) with God's written voice (the scriptures). These sustenance journals will confront, befriend and inspire you with the journal prompts and scriptures.

Arleen has been journaling for over 25 years. One of her most fondest moments is to find a quiet place (preferably near a body of water) and re-read journals past: discovering how much she has grown, needs to grow and I how grateful she is to be growing. Journaling along with her faith has helped her reach her personal and professional goals, walk through some fiery circumstances (with mind and creativity intact), forgive, live and develop a heart of gratitude. Journaling with scriptures helps her to keep God's perspective on this journey called life. Arleen desires to offer this unforgettable journaling experience to anyone who has a pen and a few minutes to use the power of their written voice to create for themselves a healthier body, mind and spirit.